The
Country
Paradise
Quilt

The
Country
Paradise
Quilt

Cheryl A. Benner
and
Rachel T. Pellman

Good Books®

Intercourse, PA 17534

Acknowledgments

Design by Cheryl A. Benner
Cover and color photography by
Jonathan Charles

The Country Paradise Quilt

© 1991 by Good Books,
Intercourse, PA 17534
International Standard Book Number:
1-56148-050-9
Library of Congress Catalog Card Number:
91-74049

Library of Congress Cataloging-in-Publication Data

Benner, Cheryl A., 1962–
    The country paradise quilt/Cheryl A. Benner and Rachel T.
Pellman.

    p.   cm.
    ISBN 1-56148-050-9 (pbk.): $12.95
    1. Quilting—Patterns.   2. Appliqué—Patterns.   I. Pellman,
Rachel T. (Rachel Thomas)   II. Title.
TT835.B352   1991
746.9′7—dc20
                                        91-74049
                                           CIP

Table of Contents

The Country Paradise Quilt

 $\mathscr{S}$ tunning and elegant, the Country Paradise quilt makes a bold statement with its graceful capturing of nature's handiwork. Its name and its style evoke images of exotic, faraway places. Three large, bright flowers stand in vivid contrast against a black background. Single iris, peony and antherium flowers, surrounded by lush foliage, create the feeling of a verdant garden. Quilting emphasizes the contours of the flowers and gives them added dimension.

This burst of color is contained within an inner border anchored at each corner by a spread fan motif. Trailing ivy winds its way around the outer borders of the quilt. A miniature version of the applique design, set inside pieced fans, graces the pillow throw. Scallops accented with points finish the edges of the quilt with an appropriate flair.

In addition to the daring Country Paradise pattern, we offer a more delicate nine-patch variation on the same theme. Here nine applique patches (like the pillow throw of the original design) are set together amid pieced fan shapes. In this arrangement the flowers seem to shimmer in a star-like aura. They are surrounded by a plain inner border and an outer border of graceful ivy.

The Country Paradise quilt can also be used to create stunning wallhangings and pillows. A single patch of the nine-patch variation would be a lovely pillow accent to use with a wallhanging made from the 48″ center of the original design.

Quilts are an expression of their makers. We hope Country Paradise inspires your creativity and adventuresome spirit. Enjoy!

How to Begin

Read the following instructions thoroughly before beginning work on your quilt.

Wash all fabrics before cutting them. This process will pre-shrink and also test them for colorfastness. If the fabric is not colorfast after one washing, repeat the washings until the water remains clear, or replace the cloth with another fabric. If fabrics are wrinkled after washing and drying, iron them before using them.

Fabrics suitable for quilting are generally lightweight, tightly woven cotton and cotton/polyester blends. They should not unravel easily and should not hold excessive wrinkles when squeezed and released. Because of the hours of time required to make a quilt, it is worth investing in high quality fabrics.

Fabric requirements given here are for standard 45″ wide fabric. If you use wider or more narrow fabrics, calculate the variations you will need.

All seams are sewn using ¼″ seam allowances. Measurements given include seam allowances except for applique pieces (See "How to Applique" section).

Applique Quilts

Preparing Background Fabric

When purchasing fabric to be used for background and borders, it is best to buy the total amount needed from one bolt of fabric. This assures that all the patches and borders are the same shade. Dye lots can vary significantly from bolt to bolt of fabric and those differences are emphasized when placed next to each other in a quilt top.

Cutting diagrams are shown to make the most efficient use of fabric. Label each piece after it is cut. Mark right and wrong sides of fabric as well.

So that you know where to place the applique pieces on the background piece, trace the applique design lightly on the right side of the background fabric before beginning to stitch. Even though the applique pieces will be laid over these markings and stitched in place, it is important to mark these lines as lightly as possible.

Making Templates

Make templates from pattern pieces printed in this book,

using material that will not wear along the edges from repeated tracing. Cardboard is suitable for pieces being traced only a few times. Plastic lids or the sides of plastic cartons work well for templates that will be used repeatedly. Quilt supply shops and art supply stores carry sheets of plastic that work well for template-making.

Quiltmaking demands precision. Remember that as you begin marking. First, test the template you have made against the original printed pattern for accuracy. Templates for piecing include seam allowances. Pieces must be cut accurately to assure their fitting together. The applique templates are given in their actual size, without seam allowances. Trace them that way. Then trace them on the right side of the fabric, but spaced far enough apart so that you can cut them approximately ¼″ outside the marked line. The traced line is the fold line indicating the exact shape of the applique piece. Since these lines will be on the right side of the fabric and will be on the folded edge, markings should be as light as possible.

Each applique piece needs to be traced separately (rather than having the fabric doubled) so the fold line is marked on each one. However, since some of the pieces face in opposite directions, half should be traced facing one way and the other half should be traced facing the opposite way (see illustration).

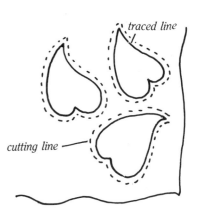

Applique templates should be traced on the right side of the fabric but spaced far enough apart so they can be cut approximately ¼″ outside the marked line.

Appliqueing

Begin by appliqueing the cut-out fabric pieces, one at a time, over the placement lines drawn onto the background fabric pieces. Be alert to the sequence in which the pieces are applied, so that sections which overlay each other are done in proper order. In cases where a portion of an applique piece is covered by another, the section being covered does not need to be stitched, since it will be held in place by the stitches of the section that overlays it.

Appliqueing is not difficult, but it does require patience and precision. The best applique work has perfectly smooth curves and sharply defined points. To achieve this, stitches must be very small and tight. First, pin the piece being appliqued to the outline on the background piece. Using thread that matches the piece being applied, stitch the piece to the background section, folding the seam allowance under to the traced line on the applique piece. Fold under only a

The applique stitch is a tiny, tight stitch that goes through the background fabric and emerges to catch only a few threads of the appliqued piece along the fold line.

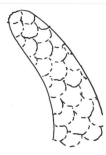

Quilting lines are marked on the surface of the quilt top. Markings should be as light as possible so they are easily seen for quilting, yet do not distract when the quilting is completed.

tiny section at a time.

The applique stitch is a running stitch going through the background fabric and emerging to catch only a few threads of the appliqued piece along the folded line. The needle should re-enter the background piece for the next stitch at almost the same place it emerged, creating a stitch so small that it is almost invisible along the edge of the appliqued piece. Stitches on the underside of the background fabric should be about ⅛″ long.

To form sharp points, fold in one side and stitch almost to the end of the point. Fold in the opposite side to form the point and push the excess seam allowance under with the point of the needle. Excess seam allowance may be trimmed to eliminate bulk. Stitch tightly.

To form smooth curves, clip along the curves to the fold line. Fold under while stitching, using the needle to push under the seam allowances.

Assembling the Appliqued Quilt Top

When all applique work is completed, the quilt is ready to be assembled. See diagram on page 15. Most applique work on the borders may be done before assembling the quilt top. However, the applique work on the corners will need to be completed after assemblage.

Quilting on Applique and Pieced Quilts
Marking Quilting Designs

Quilting designs are marked on the surface of the quilt top. A lead pencil provides a thin line and, if used with very little pressure, creates markings that are easily seen for quilting, yet do not distract when the quilt is completed. There are numerous marking pencils on the market, as well as chalk markers. Test whatever you choose on a scrap piece of fabric to be sure it performs as promised. Remember, quilting lines are not completely covered by quilting stitches, so the lines should be light or removable.

Patterns for quilting designs are included in this book. Since most spread over several pages, you will need to assemble them before using them.

Quilting

A quilt consists of three layers—the back or underside of

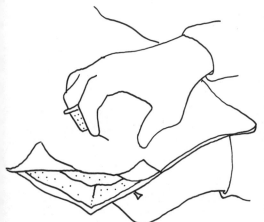

A quilt is a sandwich of three layers—the quilt back, batting and the quilt top—all held together by the quilting stitches.

the quilt, the batting, and top, which is the appliqued layer. Quilting stitches follow a decorative pattern, piercing through all three layers of the quilt "sandwich" and holding it together.

Many quilters prefer to stretch their quilts into large quilting frames. These are built so that the finished area of the quilt can be rolled up as work on it progresses. This type of frame allows space for several quilters to work on the same quilt and is used at quilting bees. Smaller hoops can also be used to quilt small sections at a time. If you use one of the smaller frames, it is important that you stretch the three layers of the quilt in the frame, then baste them securely together to prevent puckering.

The quilting stitch is a simple running stitch. Quilting needles are called "betweens" and are shorter than "sharps," which are regular hand-sewing needles. The higher the number, the smaller the needle. Many quilters prefer a size 8 or 9 needle.

Quilting is done with a single strand of quilting thread. Knot the thread and insert the needle through the top layer, about one inch away from the point where quilting should emerge on a marked quilting line. Gently tug the knot through the fabric so it is hidden between the layers. Then bring the needle up through the quilt top, going through all layers of quilt.

Keep one hand under the quilt to feel when the needle has successfully penetrated all layers and to help guide the needle back up to the surface. Your upper hand receives the needle and repeats the process. It is possible to stack as many as five stitches on the needle before pulling the thread through. However, when you work curves, you have smoother results if you stack fewer stitches. Pull the quilting stitches taut but not so tight as to pucker the fabric. When you have used the entire length of thread, reinforce the stitching with a tiny backstitch. Then reinsert the needle in the top layer, push it through for a long stitch, pull it out and clip it.

The goal in quilting is to have straight, even stitches that are of equal length on both the top and bottom of the quilt. That achievement comes with hours of practice.

When you quilt the applique patches, simply outline the applique designs. This outline quilting will accent the applique section and cause it to appear slightly puffed.

Mitering Corners

Step 1

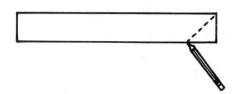

Measure in from each end the exact number of inches as the border width. Draw a diagonal line from that point to the outer corner. Cut along angled line.

Step 2

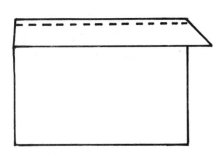

Stitch borders to quilt, leaving a ¼" seam allowance open at each mitered end.

Step 3

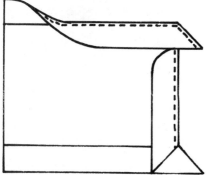

Stitch across the open ends of the corners from the inside corner to the outer edge.

Binding

The final stage in completing a quilt is the binding, which finishes the quilt's raw edge. When binding a non-straight-edged quilt, cut the binding strips on the bias. This allows more flex and stretch around curves. To cut on the bias, cut the fabric at a 45 degree angle to the straight of grain.

A double thickness of binding on the edge of the quilt gives it additional strength and durability. To create a double binding, cut the binding strips 2–2½" wide. Sew strips together to form a continuous length of binding.

When binding a quilt with scalloped edges, it is easier to attach the binding before cutting the scalloped edge. To do so, baste the raw edges of the quilt together. Mark but do not cut the scalloped border. Using a ¼" seam allowance, sew the binding along the marked edge. Pivot at the end of each point to create a sharp turn. Trim the scallops even with the edge of the binding. Wrap the binding around to the back, enclosing the raw edges and covering the stitch line. Slipstitch in place with thread that matches the color of the binding fabric.

To Display Quilts

Wall quilts can be hung in various ways. You can simply tack the quilt directly to the wall. However, this is potentially damaging to both the quilt and wall.

Another option is to hang the quilt like a painting. To do this, make a narrow sleeve from matching fabric and handsew it to the upper edge of the quilt along the back. Insert a dowel rod through the sleeve and hang the rod by wire or nylon string.

The quilt can also be hung on a frame. This method requires velcro or fabric to be attached to the frame itself. If you choose velcro, staple one side to the frame. Handsew the opposite velcro on the edge of the quilt, then attach the quilt carefully to the velcro on the frame. If you attach fabric to the frame, handstitch the quilt to the frame itself.

Quilts can also be mounted inside plexiglas by a professional framery. This method, often reserved for antique quilts, can provide an acid-free, dirt-free and, with special plexiglas, a sun-proof environment for your quilt.

Other Projects

The Country Paradise pattern is adaptable for other projects as well. To make a wallhanging, follow the instructions for appliqueing but use only the center section. Borders on wallhangings may be mitered for a more tailored look. See illustration for instructions on mitered corners.

Pillows can also be made using a single patch of the nine-patch variation. Applique the pillow top and quilt the patch. To make the back of the pillow, cut a square equal in size to the front in either matching or contrasting fabric.

Make a ruffle using one of the fabrics used in the applique design. To make the ruffle, cut three strips of fabric measuring 4½" x 45" each. Sew these strips together to form a continuous length. Bring the two ends together, wrong sides together, and stitch to create a fabric circle. Fold the fabric circle in half with wrong sides together. Stitch along the raw edge with a long running stitch around the entire circumference of the circle. Gather the circle to fit around the edges of the quilted top. Pin the ruffle to the pillow top with the raw edges even and spread the gathers evenly throughout. Baste ruffle to pillow top.

With right sides together and the ruffle sandwiched between the layers, pin back to pillow top. Stitch back to top through all layers, leaving a five-inch opening along one side. Trim seams. Turn pillow right side out. Stuff pillow with polyester fiberfil. Slipstitch opening.

Signing and Dating Quilts

To preserve history for future generations, sign and date the quilts you make. Include your initials and the year the quilt was made. This date is usually added discreetly in a corner of the quilt. It can be embroidered or quilted among the quilting designs. Another alternative is to stitch or write the information on a separate piece of fabric and handstitch it to the back of the quilt. Whatever method you choose, this is an important part of finishing your quilt.

The Country Paradise Quilt
Cutting Layout for Queen-size or Double-size Quilt
Final Size—approximately 94" x 111"
(Measurements include seam allowances)

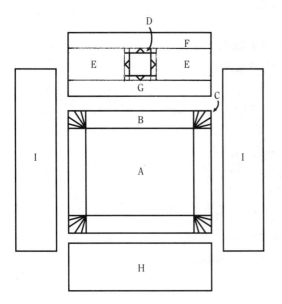

A. **Center Square**—48½" square (standard 45" wide fabric will require piecing of this center square)
B. **Inner Border**—cut four—6½" x 48½"
C. **Shaded Fan**—Templates given (C1, C2, C3)
D. **Small Shaded Fan**—Templates given for piecing (D1, D2, D3, D4, D5); applique is done on a 10½" square
E. **Pillow Throw Side Sections**—cut two—16½" x 22"
F. **Pillow Throw Top Section**—cut one—7½" x 60½"

G. **Pillow Throw Lower Section**—cut one—11½" x 60½"
H. **Bottom Border**—cut one—17" x 60½"
I. **Side Borders**—cut two—17" x 111"

Yardage for Piecing of The Country Paradise Quilt

A. 3 yards of 45" fabric (use remaining fabric for 10½" square on Pillow Throw)

B. 1½ yards
- C1, D1—use fabric left over from B
- C2, D2—¼ yard
- C3, D3—¼ yard
- D4, D5, E, F, G, H, I—5½ yards (see diagram for cutting layout of E through I)

17"x111" ⓘ	17"x60½" Ⓗ	16½"x22" Ⓔ
17"x111" ⓘ	11½"x60½" Ⓖ	16½"x22" Ⓔ
Ⓕ 7½"x60½"		

- Binding—1 yard

Yardage for Applique for The Country Paradise Quilt

Peony Flower print fabric—⅞ yard
Peony Flower solid fabric—¾ yard
Iris Flower dark fabric—⅜ yard
Iris Flower light fabric—¾ yard
Antherium Flower print fabric—⅞ yard
Antherium Flower solid fabric—⅞ yard
Flower Centers/Accents
  on Iris Flower—¼ yard
Ivy Leaf and Stems—1½ yards
Ivy Leaf Accent—¾ yard
Broad Leaf and Stems—⅜ yard
Broad Leaf Accent—¼ yard

The Country Paradise Nine-Patch Variation Quilt
Cutting Layout for Queen-size or Double-Size Quilt

Final Size—approximately 94" x 111"
(Measurements include seam allowances)

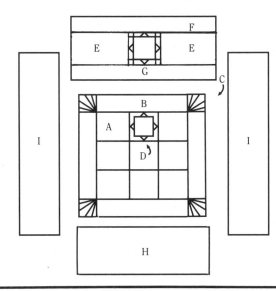

A. Background and Pillow Throw Patch—cut 10—10½" squares

B. Inner Border—cut 4—6½" x 48½"

C. Shaded Fan—Templates given (C1, C2, C3)

D. Small Shaded Fan—Templates given (D1, D2, D3, D4, D5)

E. Pillow Throw Side Sections—cut 2—16½" x 22"

F. Pillow Throw Top Section—cut 1—7½" x 60½"

G. Pillow Throw Lower Section—cut 1—11½" x 60½"

H. Bottom Border—cut 1—17" x 60½"

I. Side Borders—cut 2—17" x 111"

Yardage for Piecing of The Country Paradise Nine Patch Variation Quilt

A. 1 yard

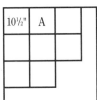

B. 1½ yards
- C1, D1—Use fabric leftover from B
- C2, D2—¾ yard
- C3, D3—¾ yard
- D4, 5, E, F, G, H, I—6 yards (See diagram from original Country Paradise Quilt for fabric layouts of E through I)

Yardage for Applique for The Country Nine Patch Variation Quilt

Peony Flower print fabric—½ yard
Peony Flower solid fabric—¼ yard
Iris Flower dark fabric—¼ yard
Iris Flower light fabric—¼ yard
Antherium Flower print fabric—¼ yard
Antherium Flower solid fabric—⅓ yard
Flower Centers/Accents on
Iris Flower—⅛ yard
Ivy Leaf and Stems—1¼ yards
Ivy Leaf Accent—¾ yard
Broad Leaf/Stems—⅛ yard
Broad Leaf Accent—⅛ yard

Assembly Instructions for the Country Paradise Nine-Patch Variation Quilt
Queen-size/Double-size

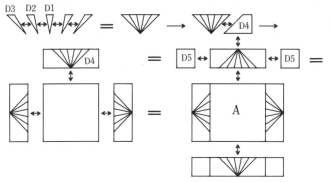

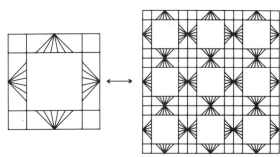

Follow remaining assembly instructions from the original Country Paradise Quilt

Assembly Instructions for the Country Paradise Quilt
Queen-size/Double-size

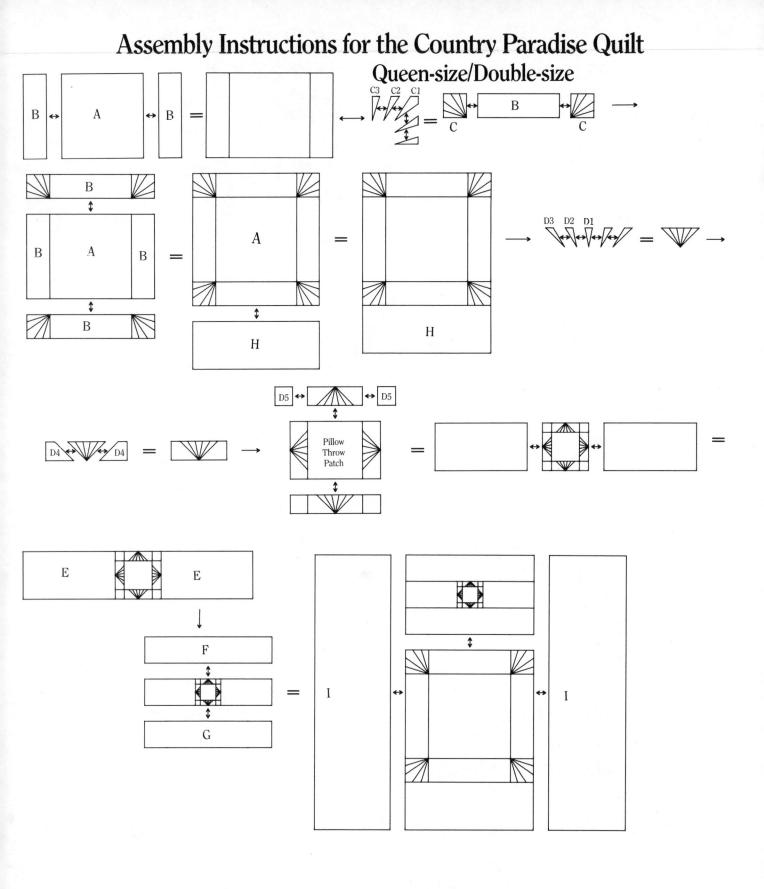

The Country Paradise Quilt Applique Templates
Outer Peony Flower

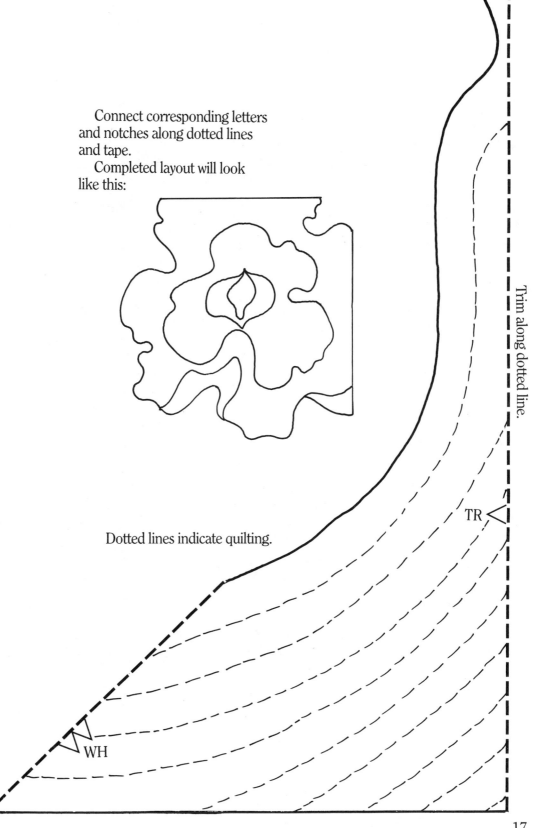

Connect corresponding letters and notches along dotted lines and tape.

Completed layout will look like this:

Dotted lines indicate quilting.

Trim along dotted line.

TR

WH

The Country Paradise Quilt Applique Templates
Outer Peony Flower

WH

WF

Trim along dotted line.

WG

Peony Flower Accent
Ⓑ

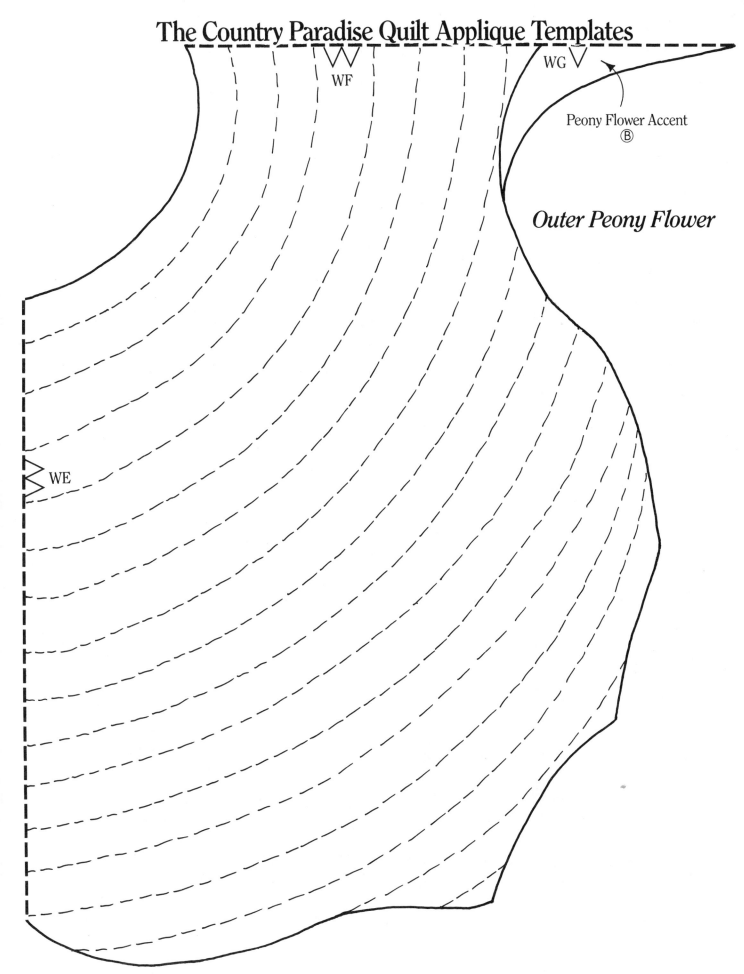

WF

WG

Peony Flower Accent
Ⓑ

Outer Peony Flower

WE

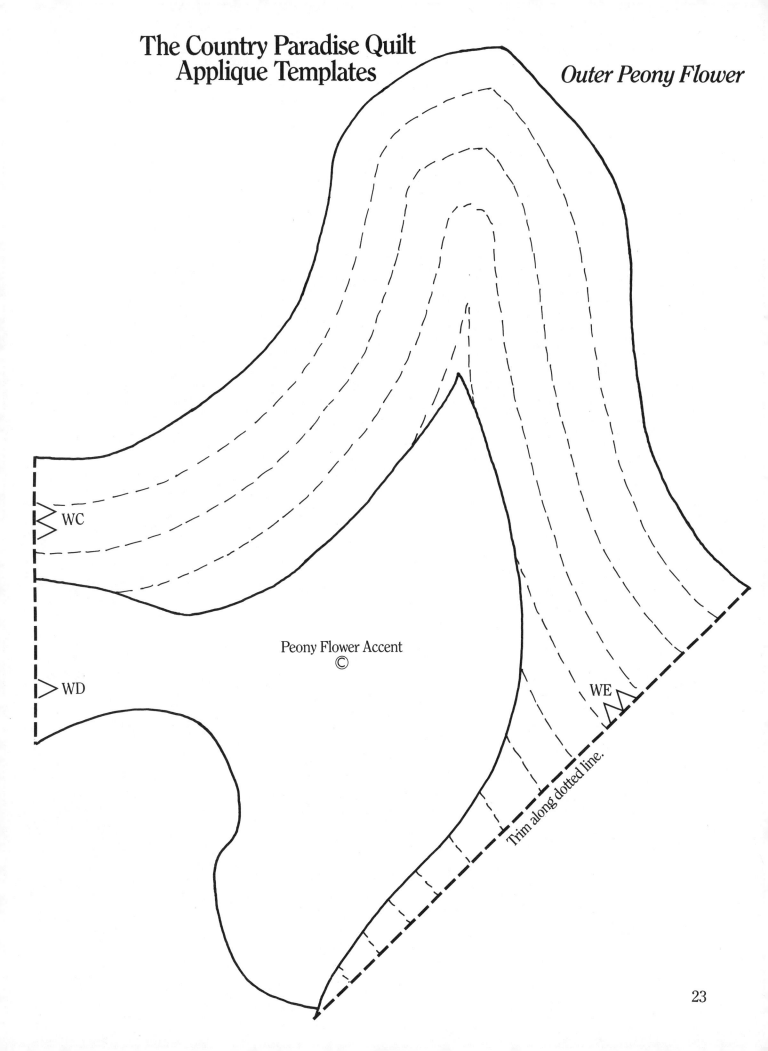

The Country Paradise Quilt
Applique Templates

Outer Peony Flower

WC

WD

Peony Flower Accent
©

WE

Trim along dotted line.

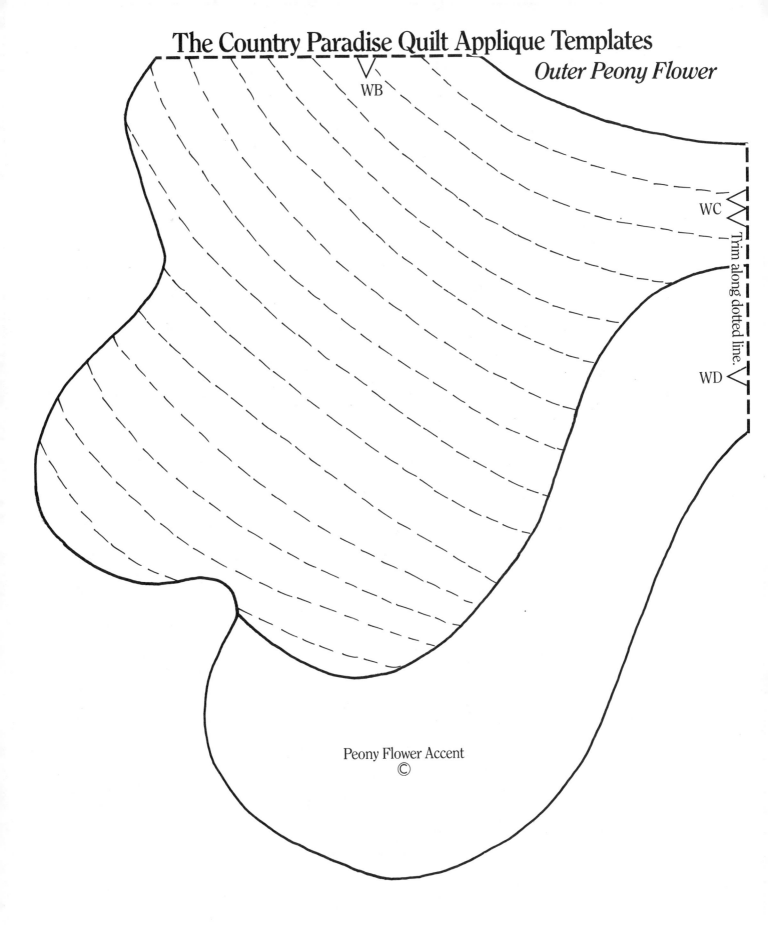

WB

WC

WD

Trim along dotted line.

Peony Flower Accent
©

Outer Peony Flower

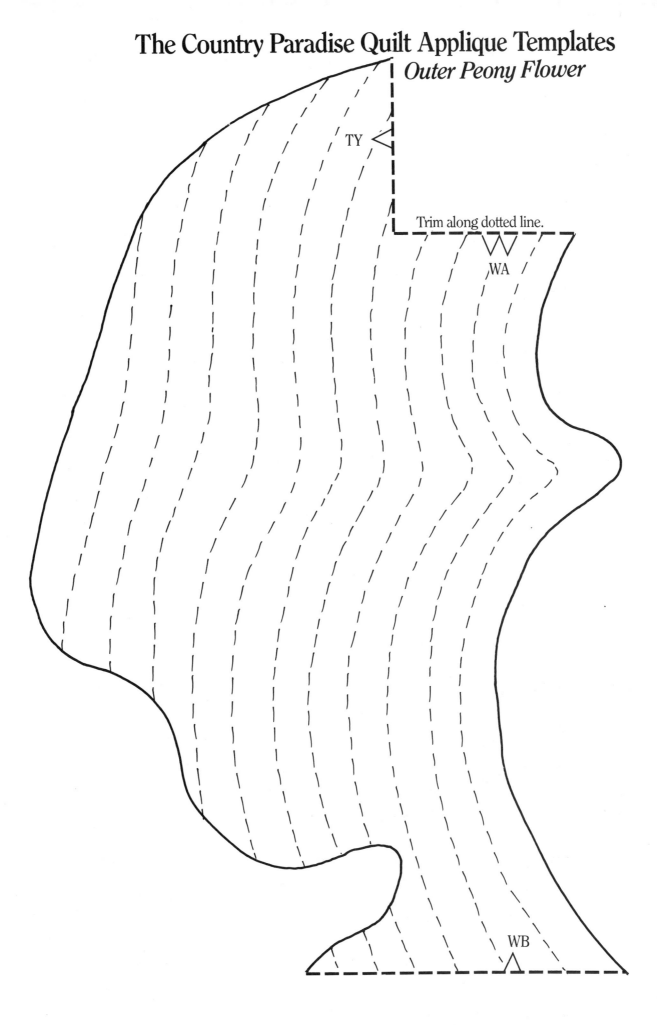

TY

Trim along dotted line.

WA

WB

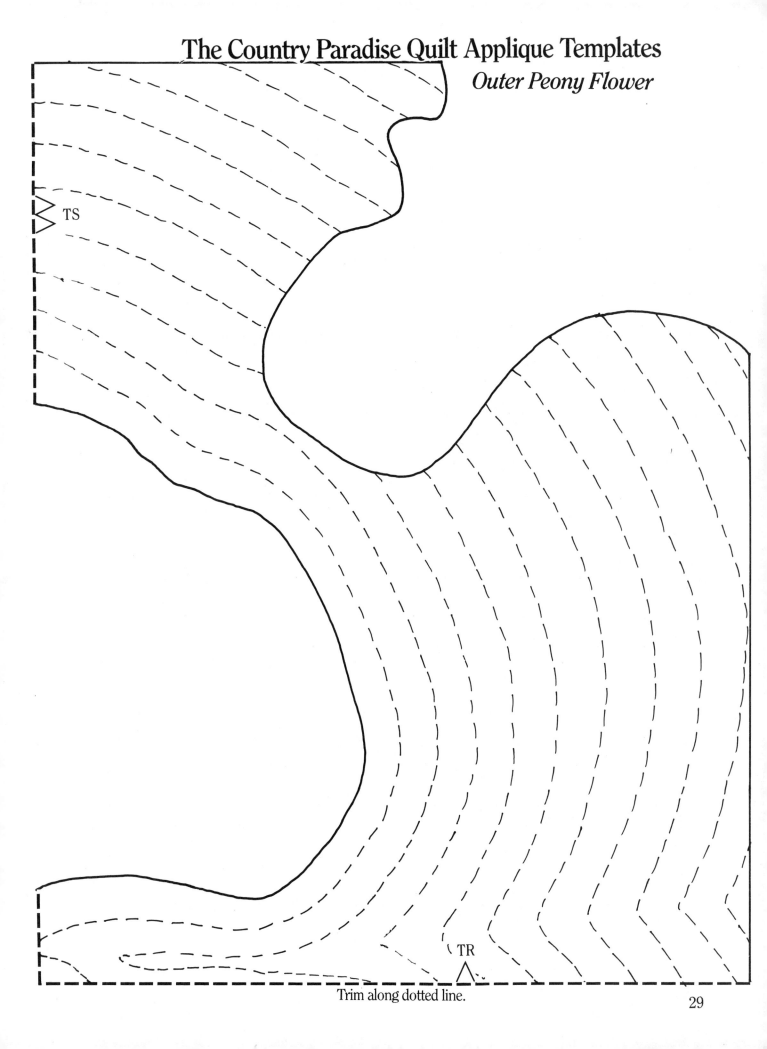

The Country Paradise Quilt Applique Templates
Outer Peony Flower

TS

TR

Trim along dotted line.

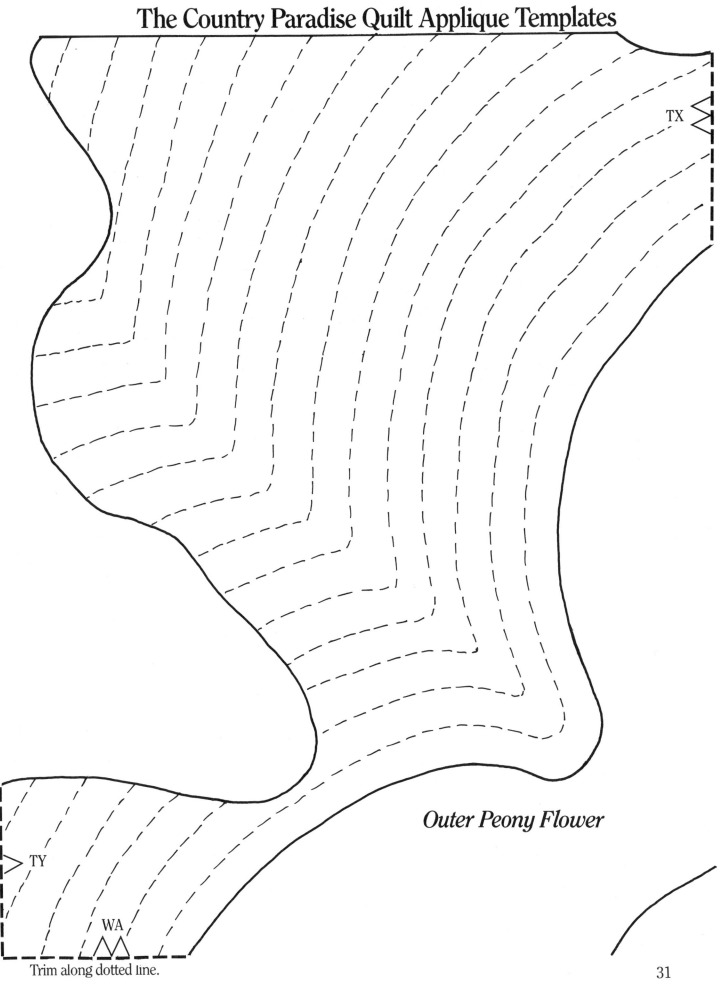

TX

Outer Peony Flower

TY

WA

Trim along dotted line.

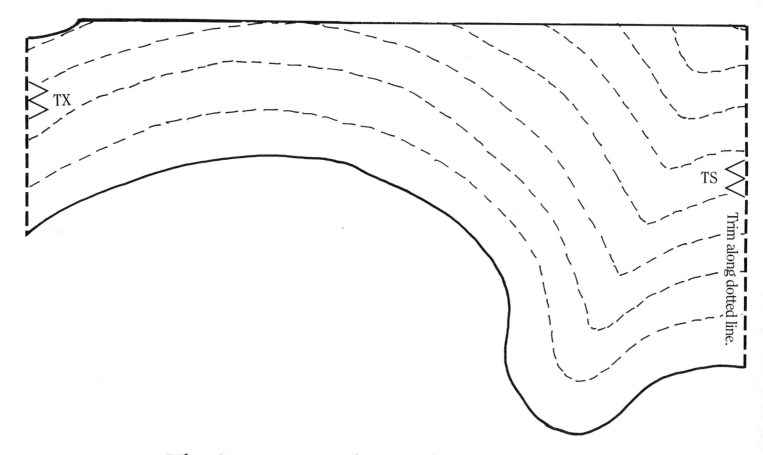

TX

TS

Trim along dotted line.

The Country Paradise Quilt Applique Templates
Outer Peony Flower

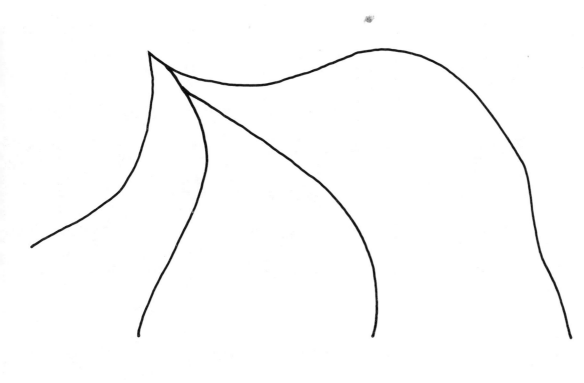

The Country Paradise Quilt Applique Templates
Peony Flower Stem

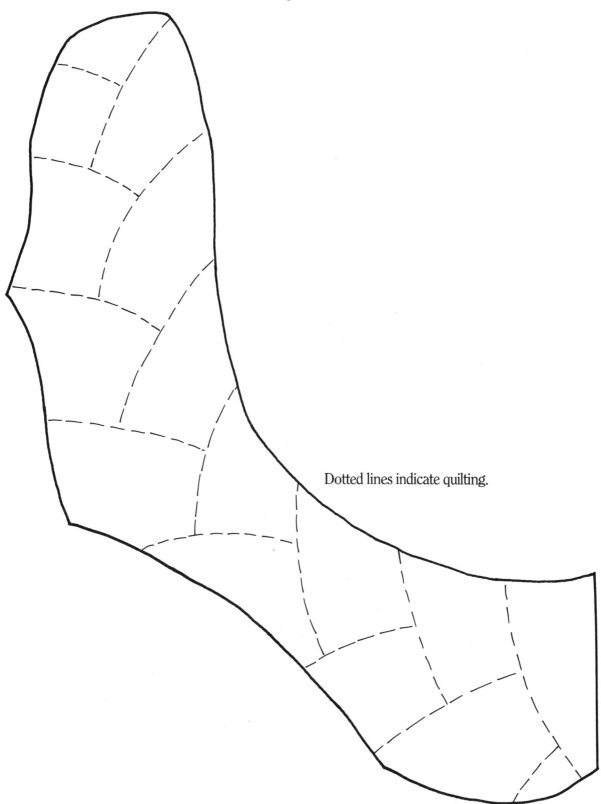

Dotted lines indicate quilting.

The Country Paradise Quilt Applique Templates

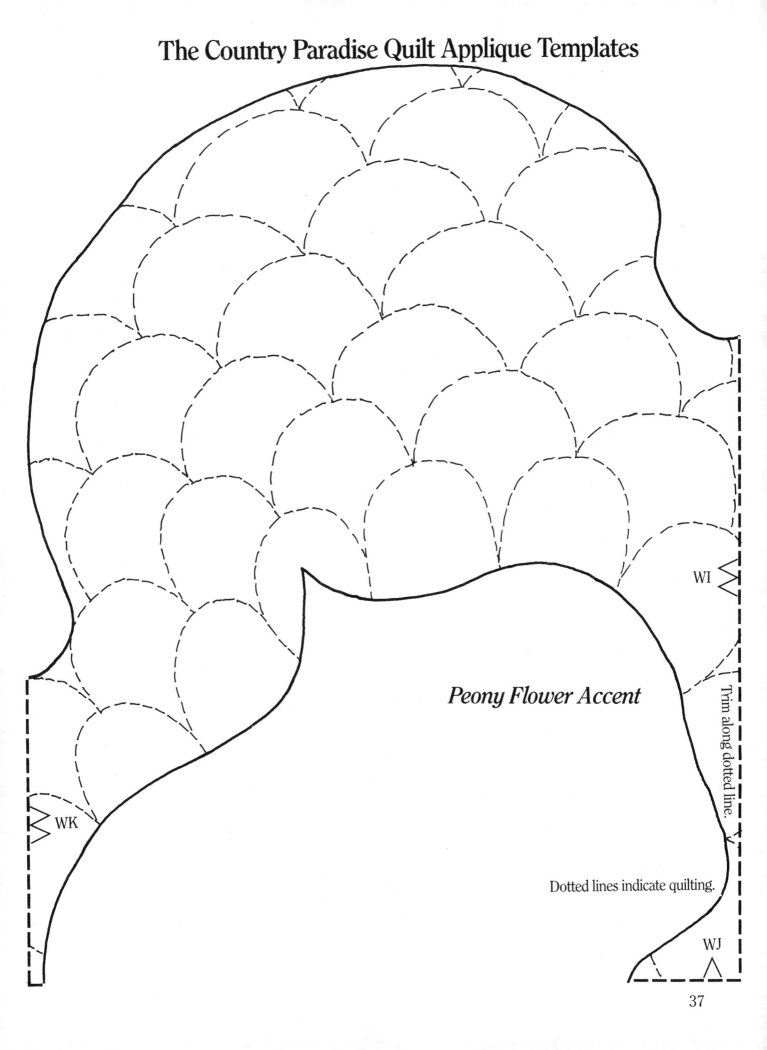

Peony Flower Accent

WI

Trim along dotted line.

WK

Dotted lines indicate quilting.

WJ

The Country Paradise Quilt Applique Templates
Peony Flower Accent

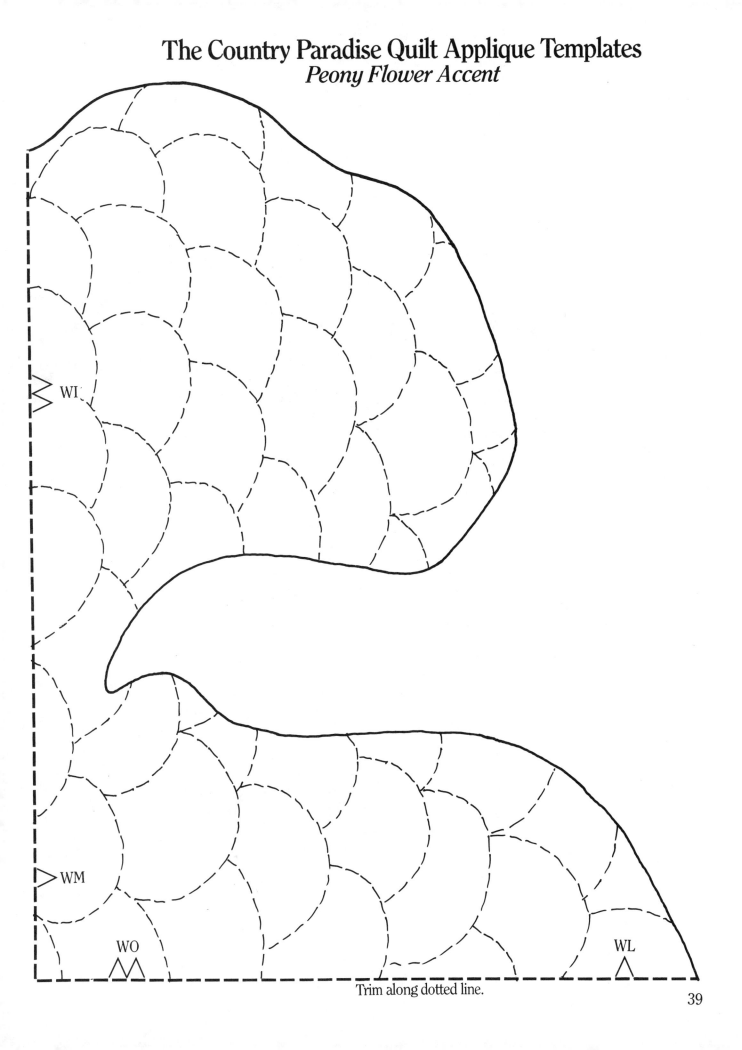

WI

WM

WO

WL

Trim along dotted line.

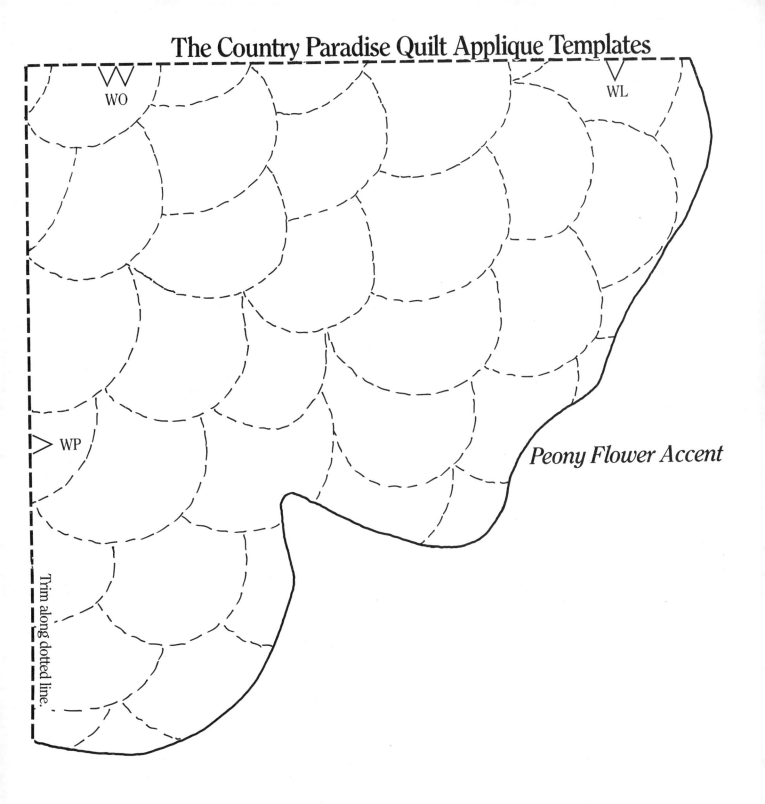

WO

WL

WP

Peony Flower Accent

Trim along dotted line.

The Country Paradise Quilt Applique Templates
Peony Flower Accent

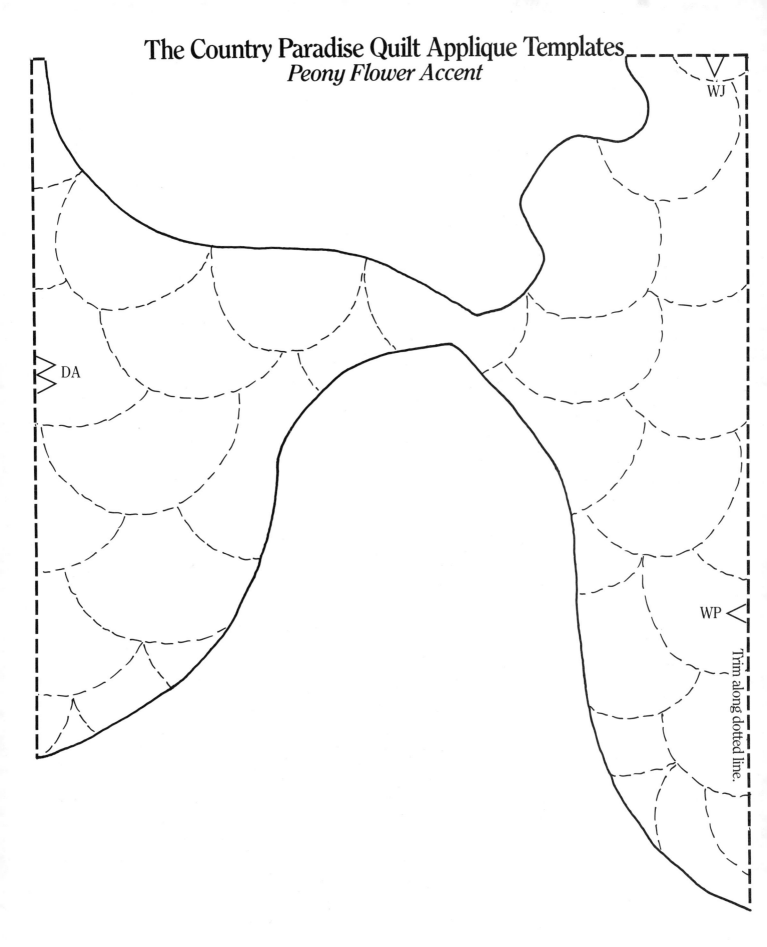

DA

WJ

WP

The Country Paradise Quilt Applique Templates
Peony Flower Accent

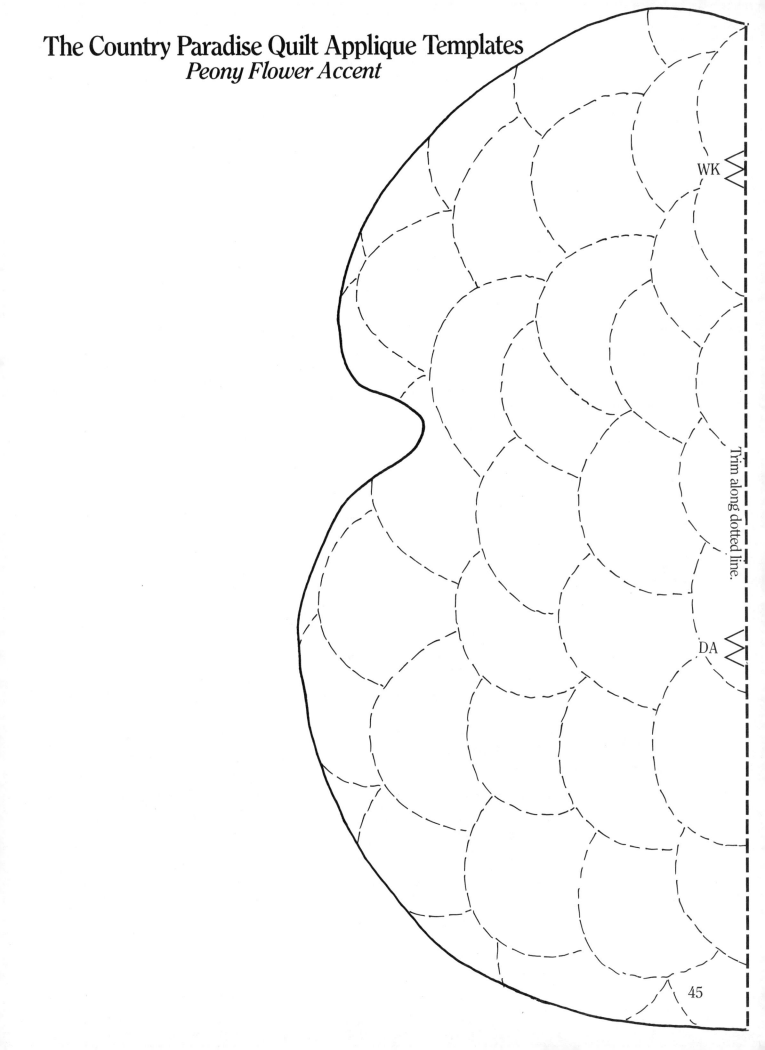

WK

Trim along dotted line.

DA

45

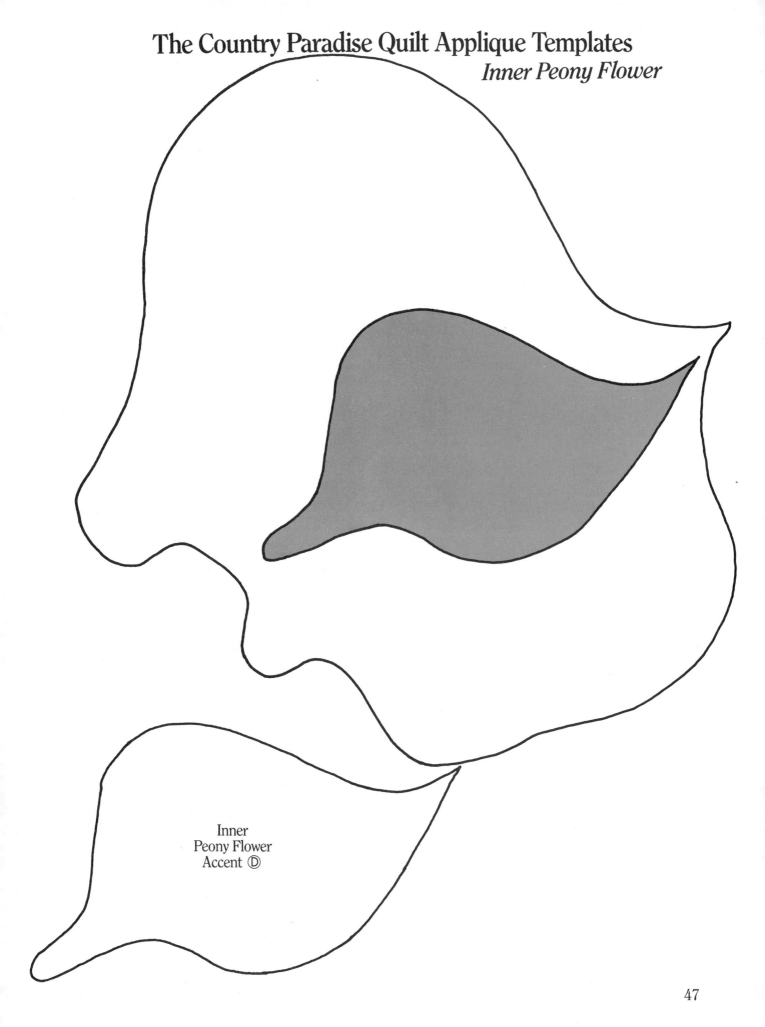

The Country Paradise Quilt Applique Templates
Inner Peony Flower

Inner
Peony Flower
Accent Ⓓ

The Country Paradise Quilt Applique Templates
Ivy Leaf Stems

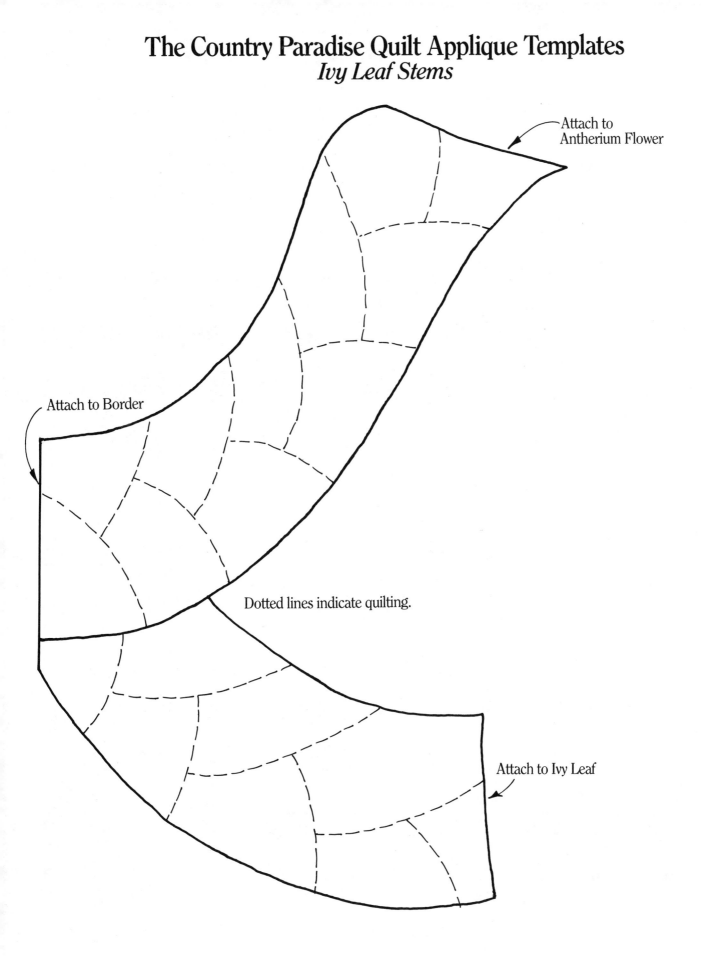

Attach to
Antherium Flower

Attach to Border

Dotted lines indicate quilting.

Attach to Ivy Leaf

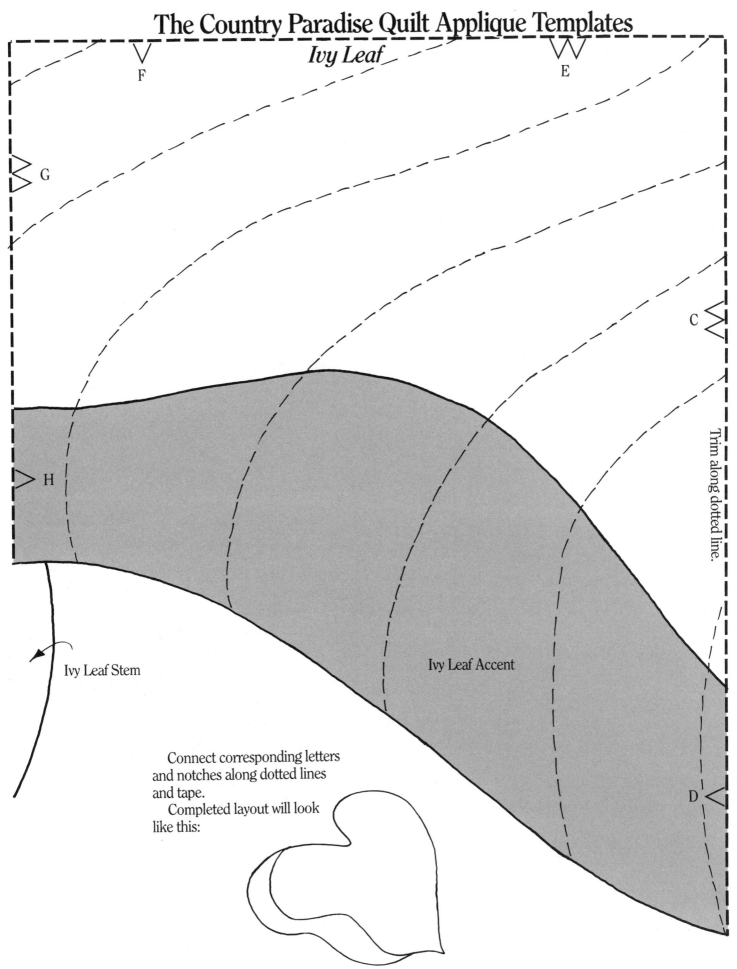

Ivy Leaf

F

E

G

C

Trim along dotted line.

H

Ivy Leaf Stem

Ivy Leaf Accent

D

Connect corresponding letters
and notches along dotted lines
and tape.

Completed layout will look
like this:

Ivy Leaf

A

B

C

Trim along dotted line.

Dotted lines indicate quilting.

D

Ivy Leaf Accent

The Country Paradise Quilt Applique Templates
Ivy Leaf

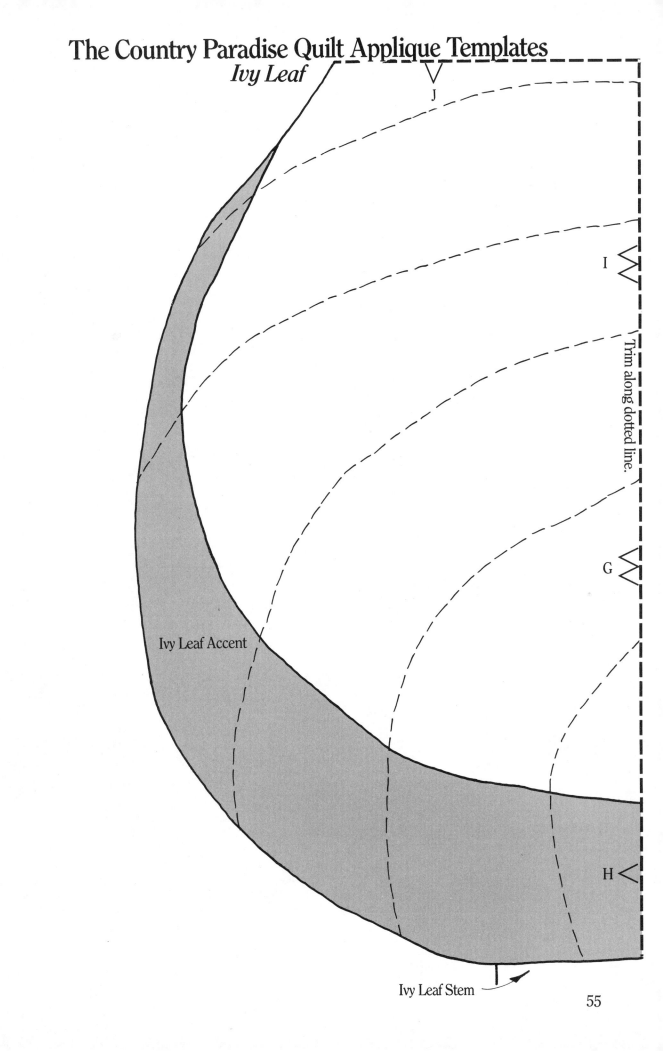

J

I

Trim along dotted line.

G

Ivy Leaf Accent

H

Ivy Leaf Stem

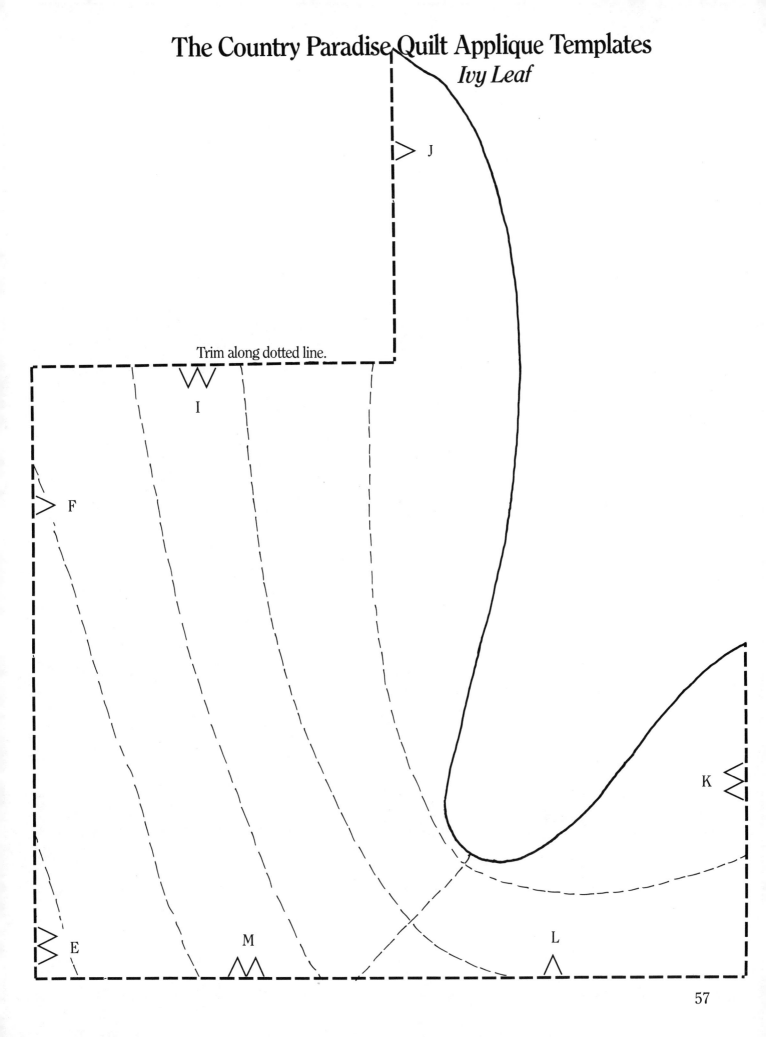

Trim along dotted line.

The Country Paradise Quilt Applique Templates
Ivy Leaf

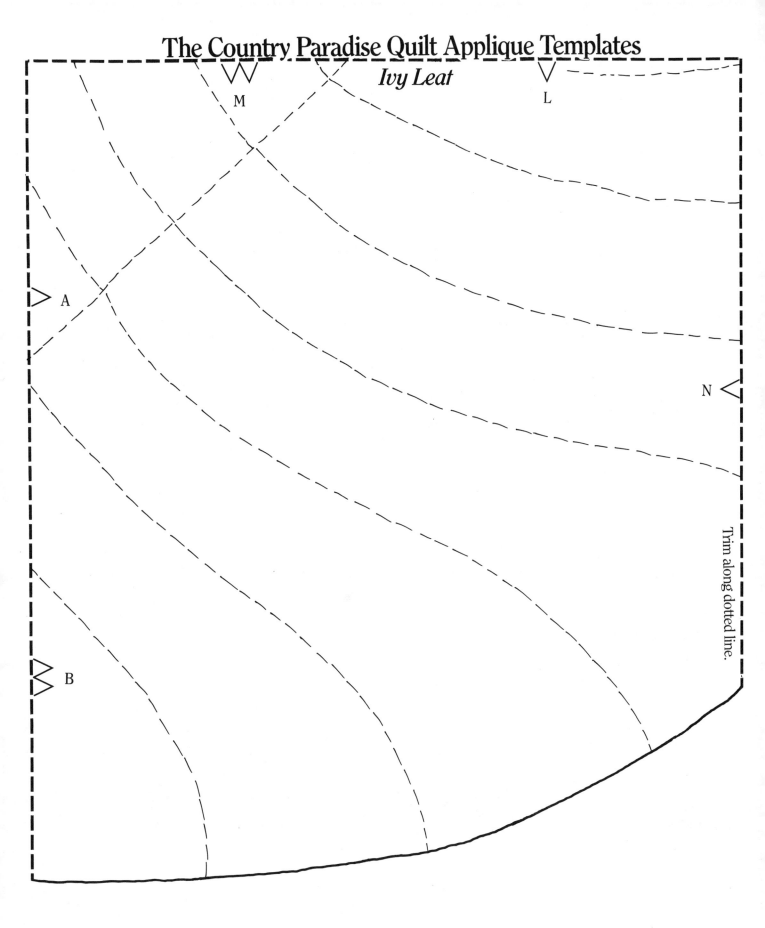

A

B

M

L

N

Trim along dotted line.

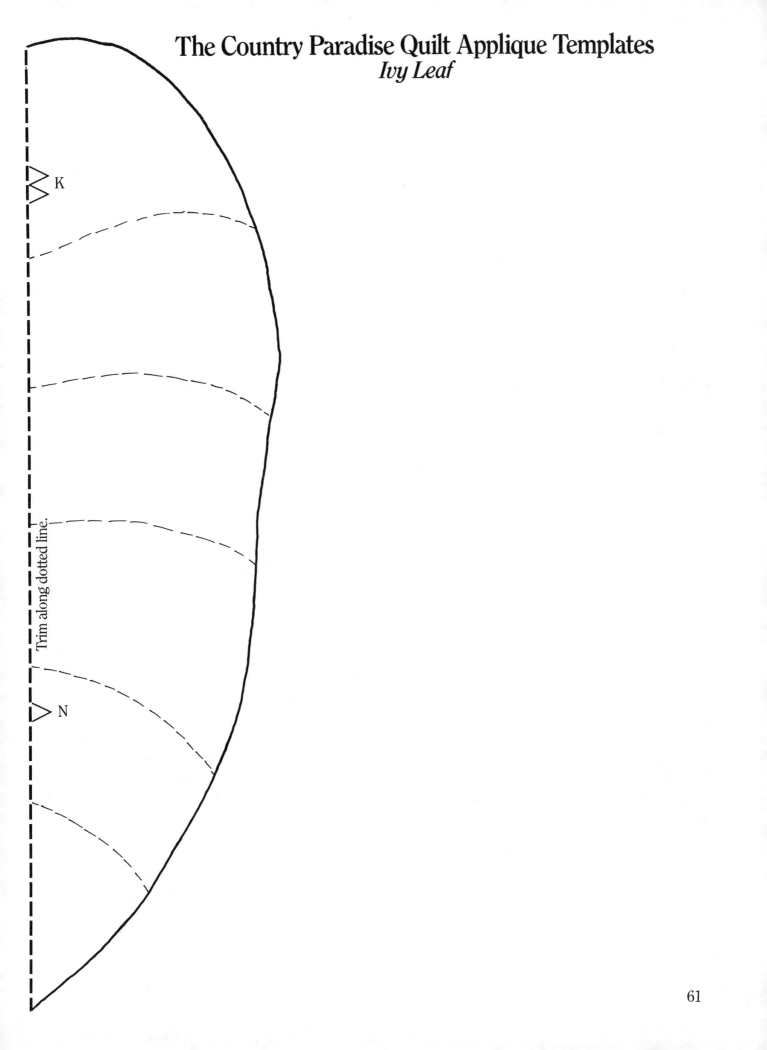

The Country Paradise Quilt Applique Templates
Ivy Leaf

K

Trim along dotted line.

N

Broad Leaf II

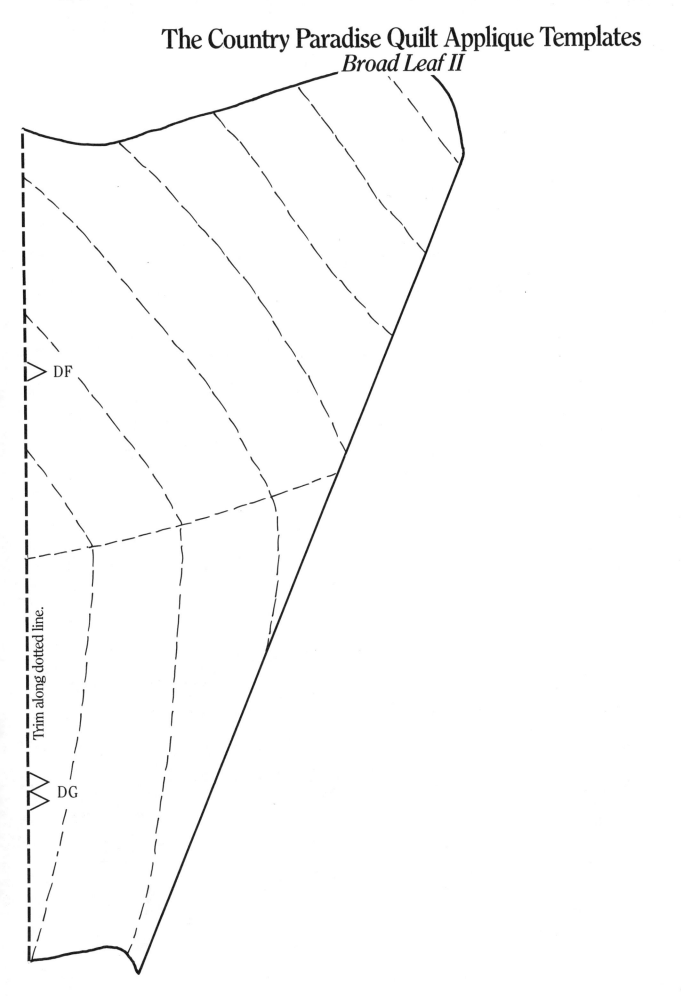

DF

DG

Trim along dotted line.

The Country Paradise Quilt Applique Templates
Broad Leaf II

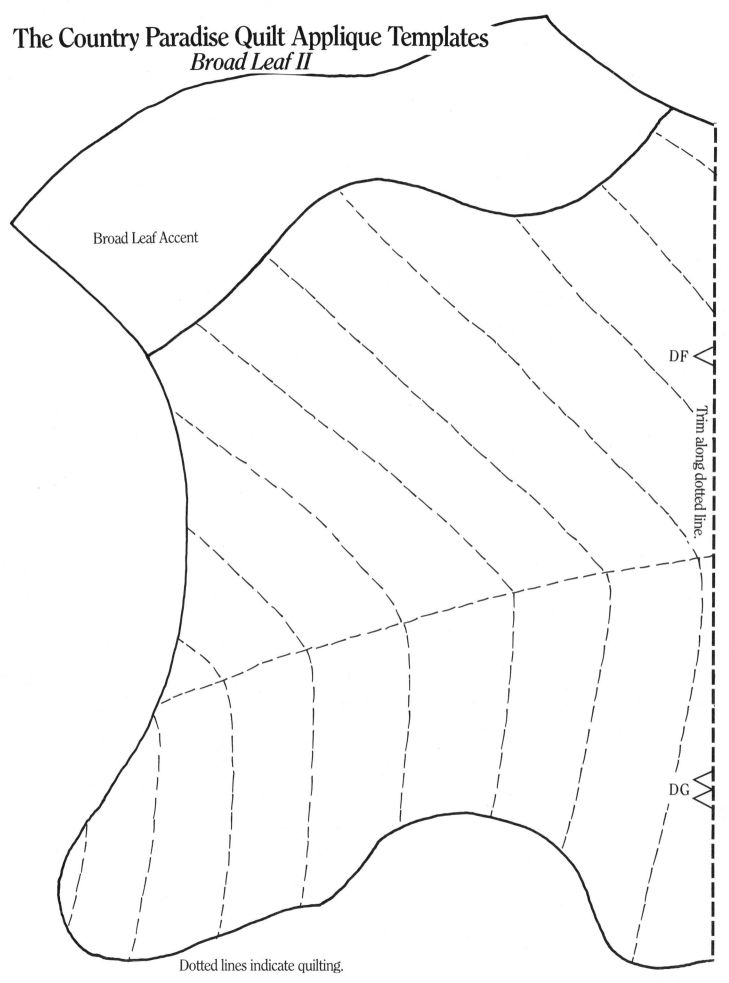

Broad Leaf Accent

DF

Trim along dotted line.

DG

Dotted lines indicate quilting.

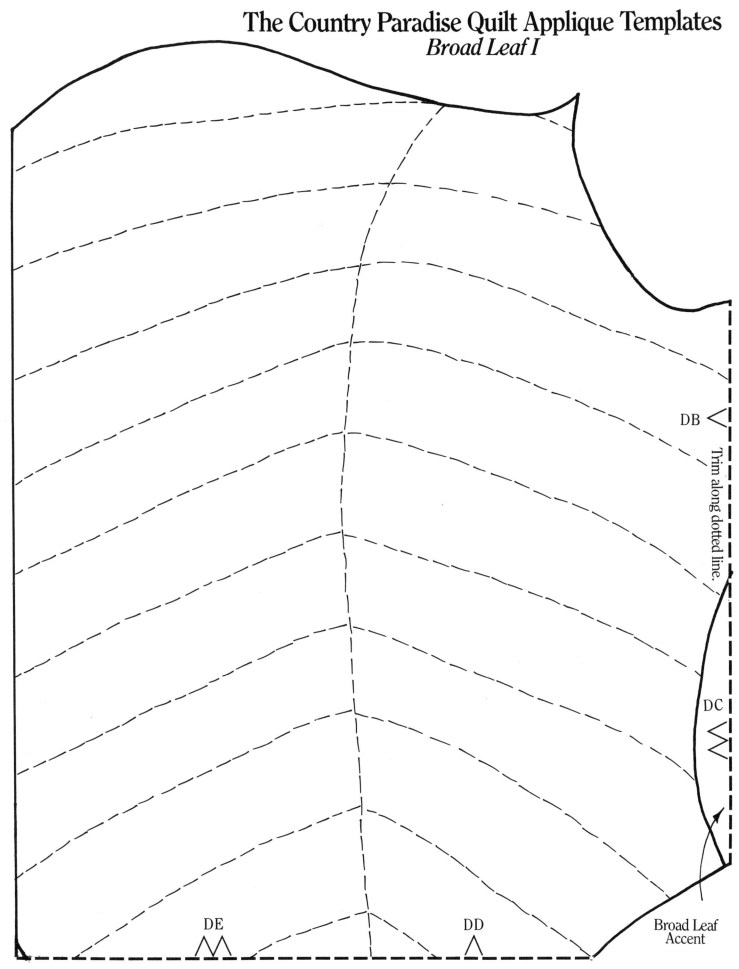

DB

Trim along dotted line.

DC

DE

DD

Broad Leaf
Accent

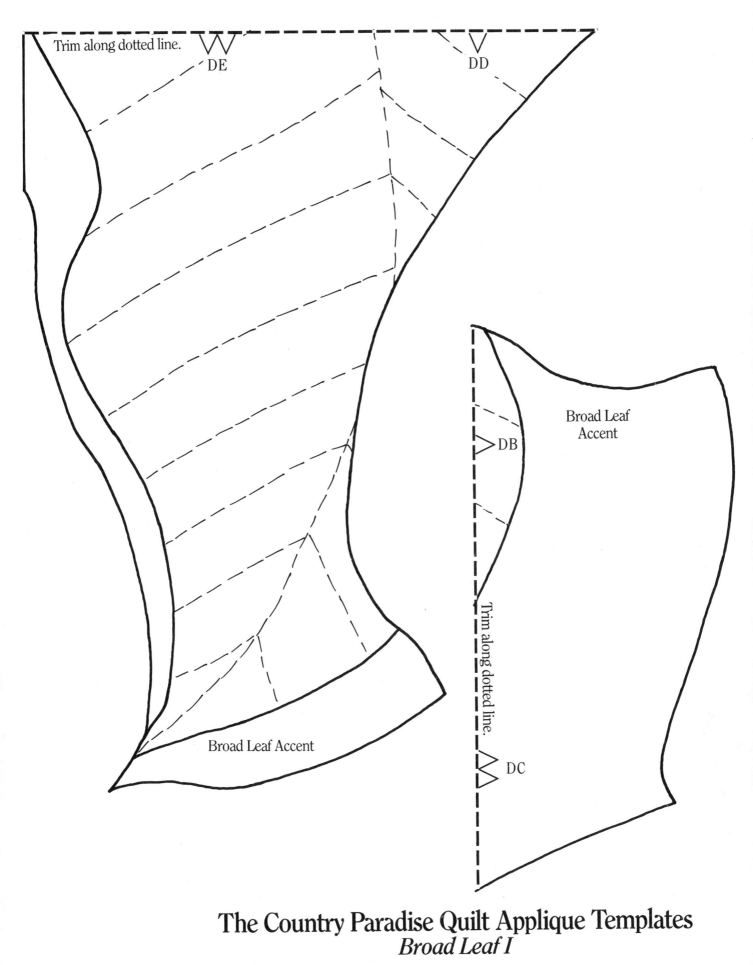

Trim along dotted line.

DE

DD

DB

Broad Leaf
Accent

Trim along dotted line.

DC

Broad Leaf Accent

The Country Paradise Quilt Applique Templates
Broad Leaf I

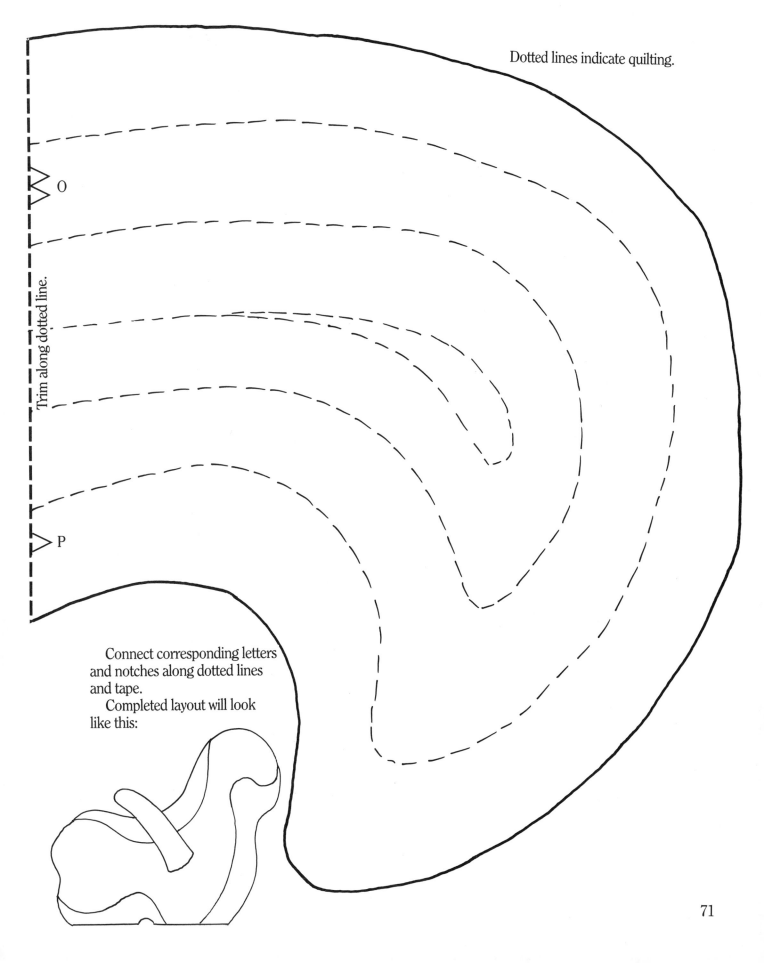

The Country Paradise Quilt Applique Template
Antherium Flower

Dotted lines indicate quilting.

Trim along dotted line.

O

P

Connect corresponding letters
and notches along dotted lines
and tape.
Completed layout will look
like this:

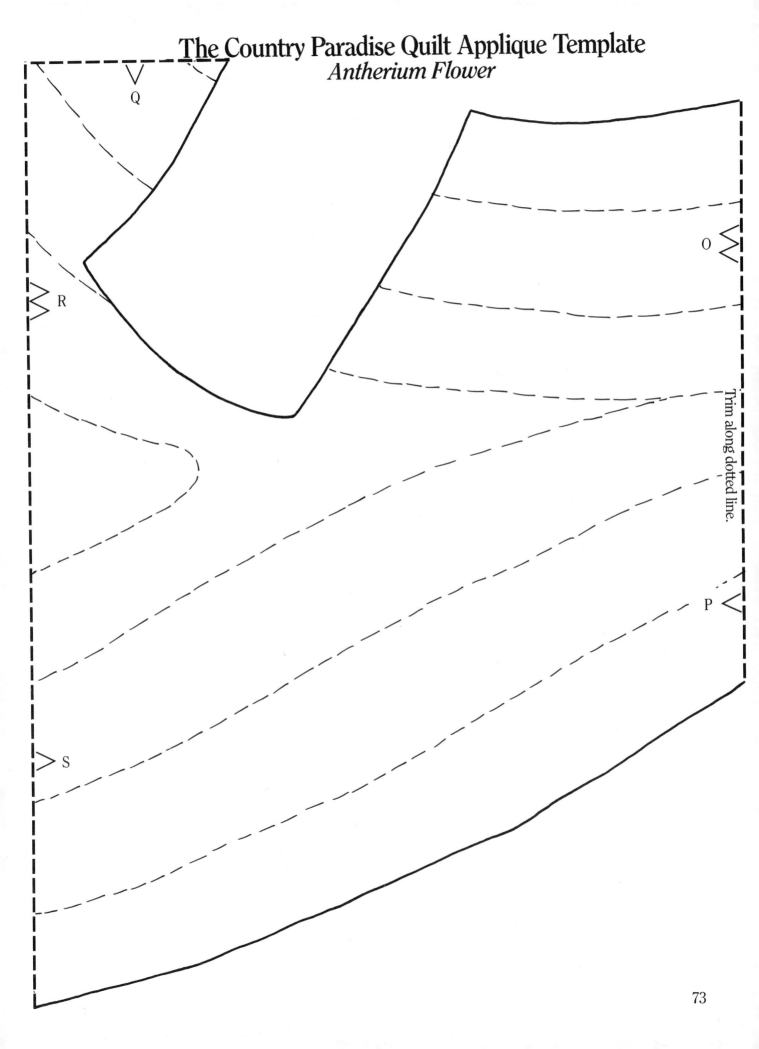

Q

R

O

S

Trim along dotted line.

P

The Country Paradise Quilt Applique Template
Antherium Flower

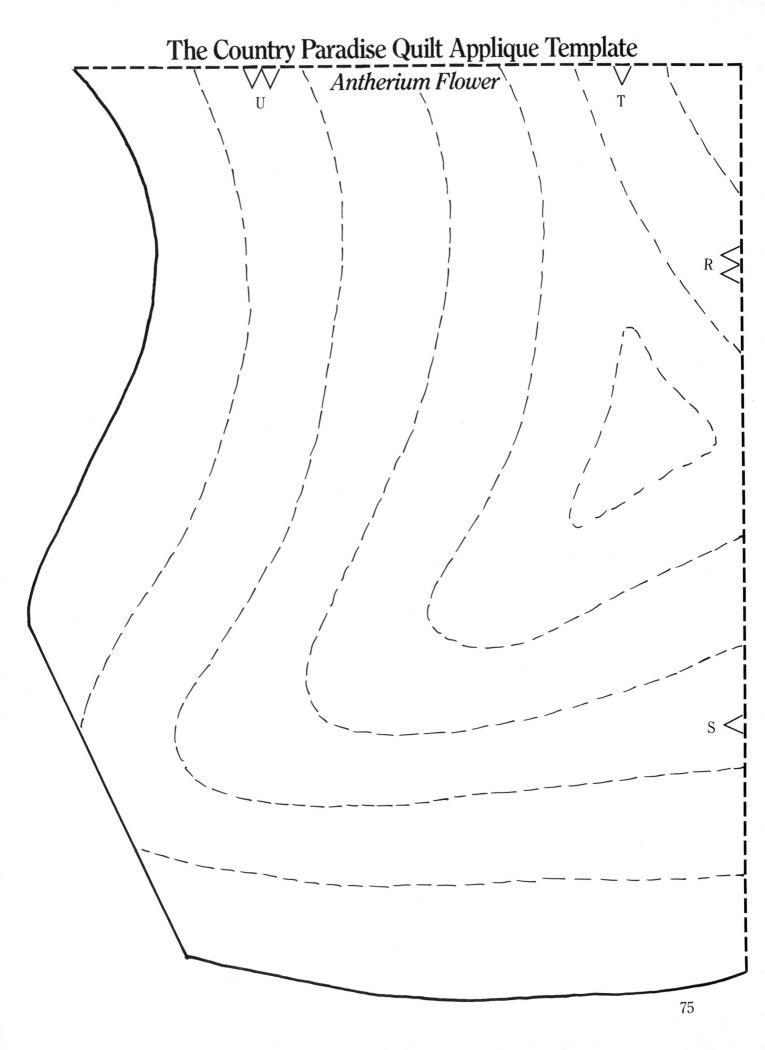

U

T

R

S

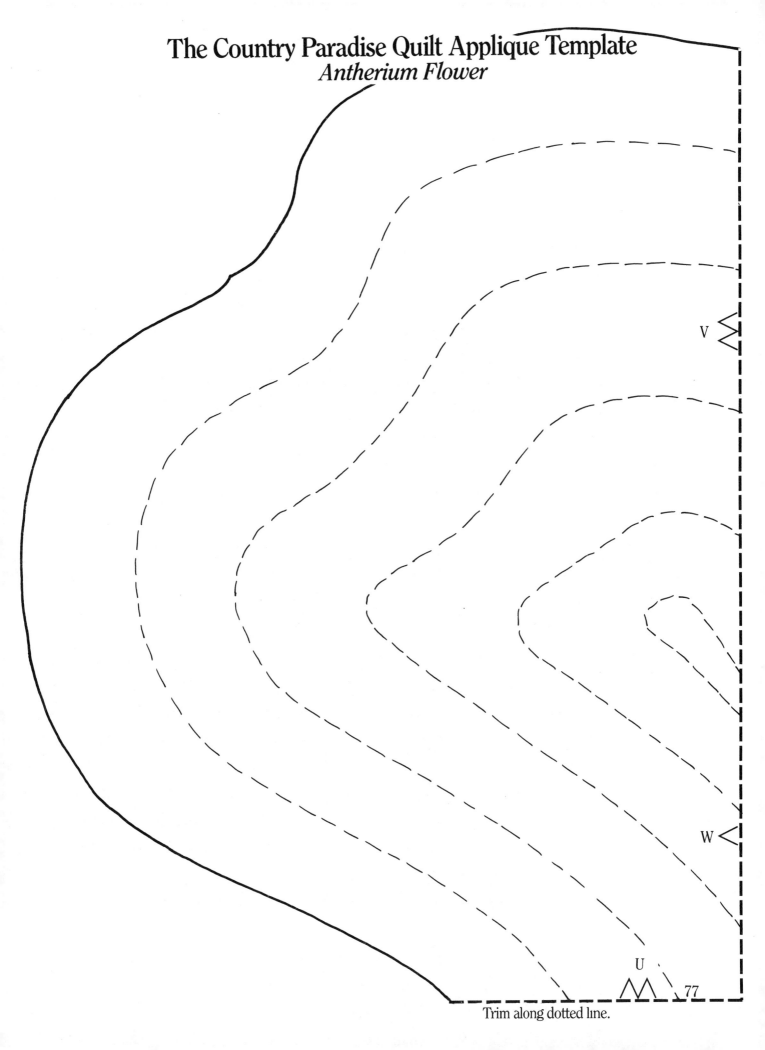

The Country Paradise Quilt Applique Template
Antherium Flower

V

W

U

77

Trim along dotted line.

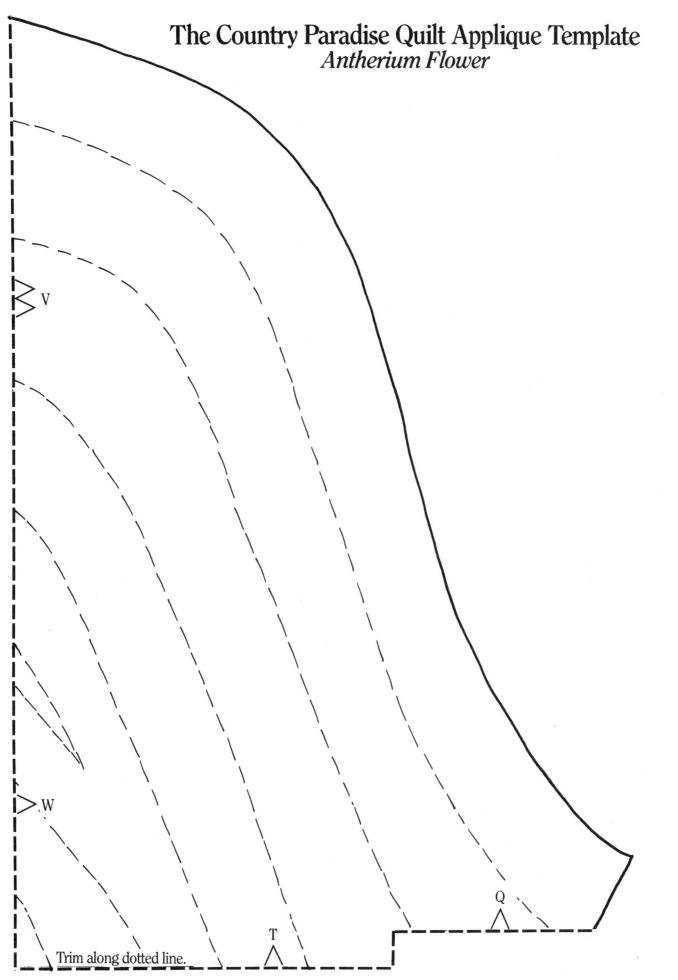

The Country Paradise Quilt Applique Template
Antherium Flower

V

W

Q

T

Trim along dotted line.

The Country Paradise Quilt Applique Templates
Antherium Flower Accent

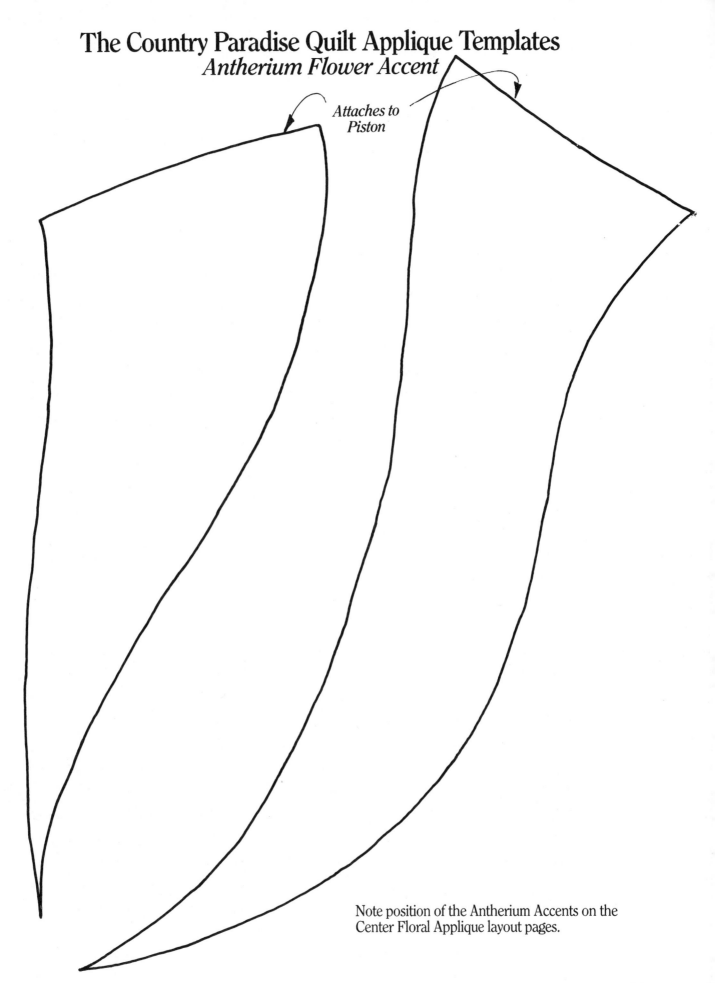

Attaches to Piston

Note position of the Antherium Accents on the Center Floral Applique layout pages.

The Country Paradise Quilt Applique Templates
Antherium Flower Accent

X

X

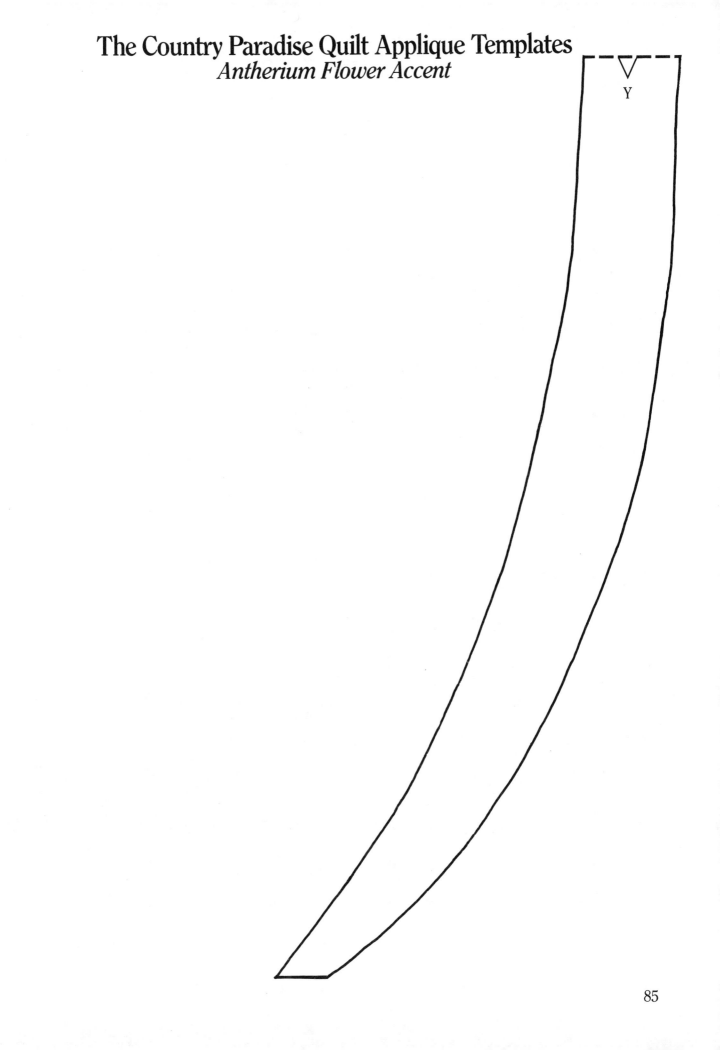

Y

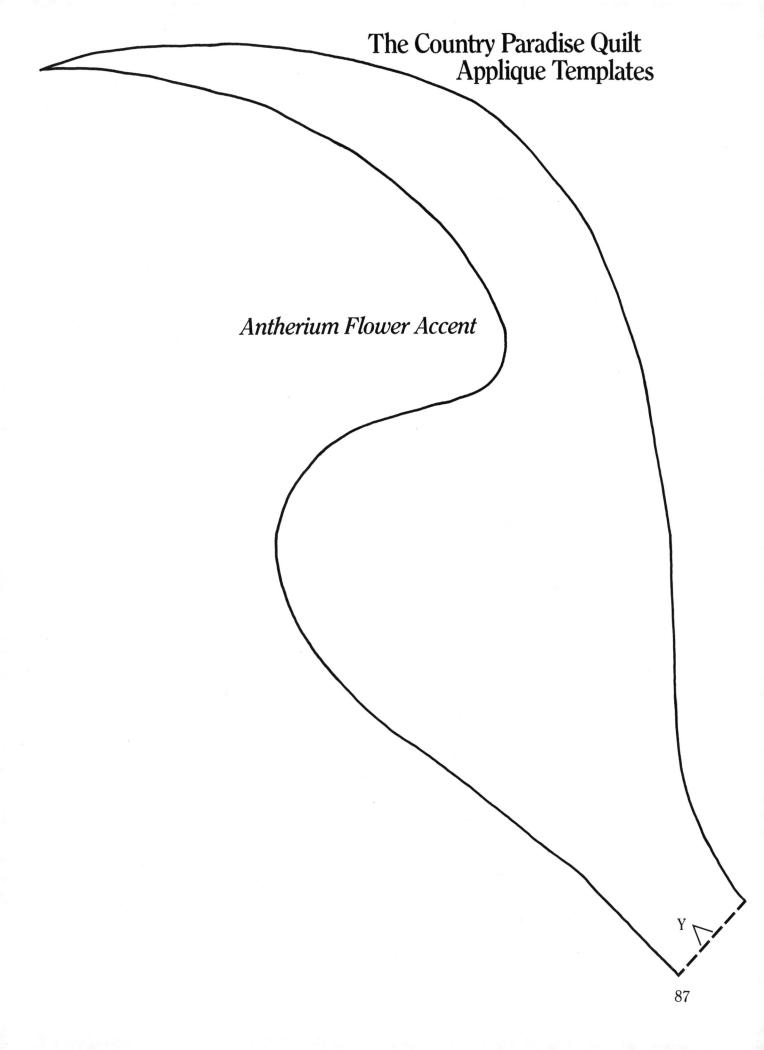

Antherium Flower Accent

Y

The Country Paradise Quilt Applique Template
Piston

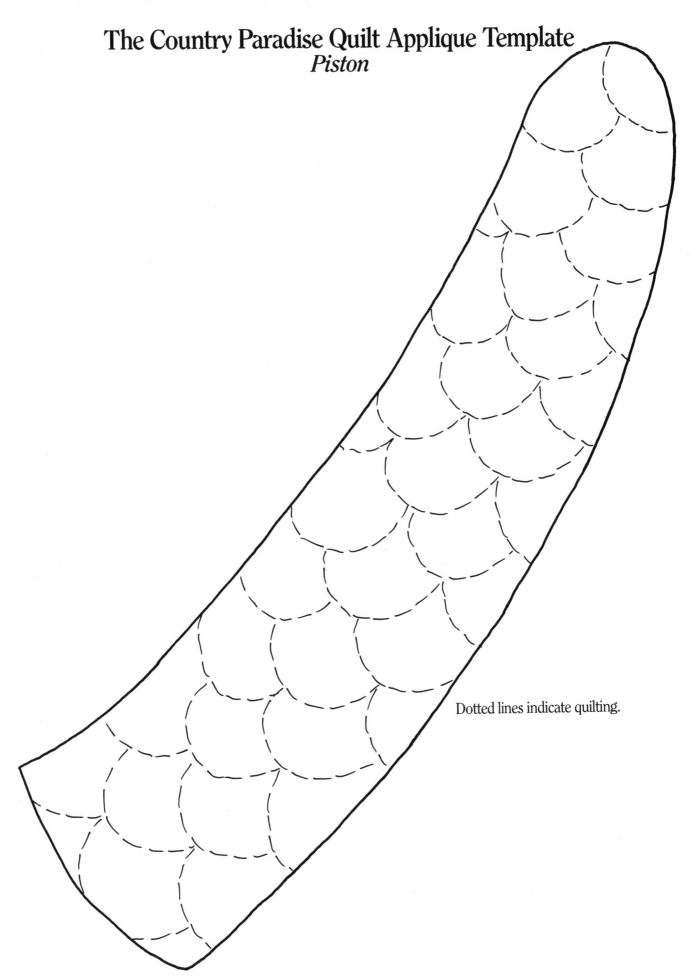

Dotted lines indicate quilting.

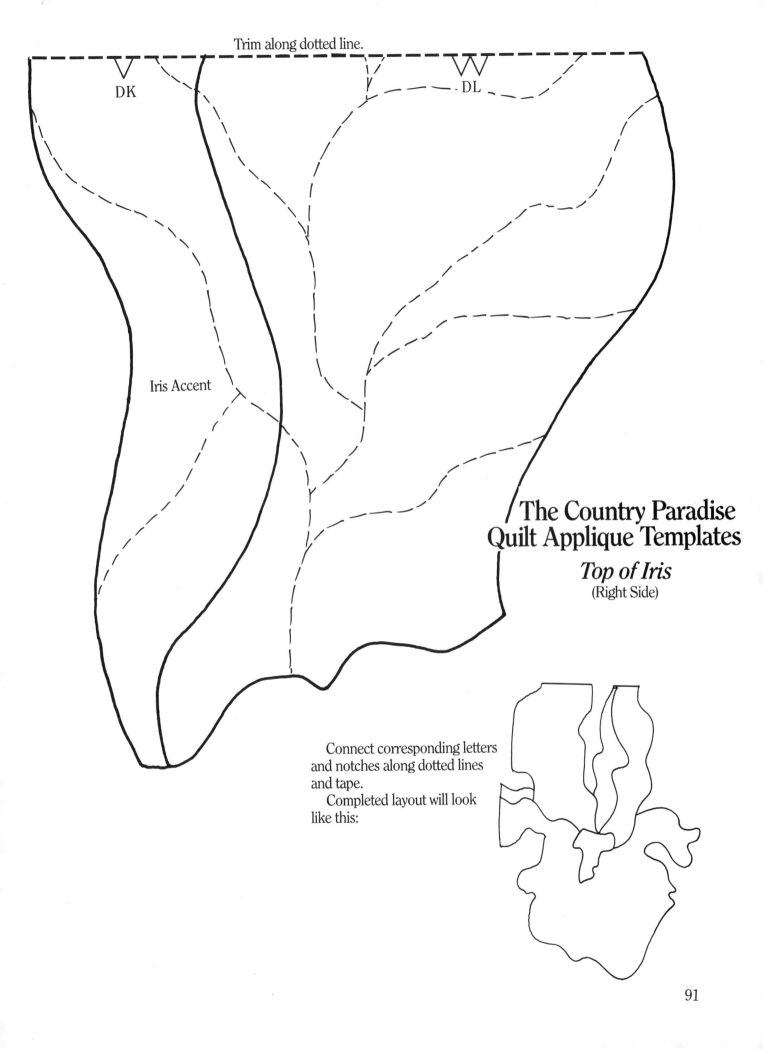

Trim along dotted line.

DK

DL

Iris Accent

The Country Paradise
Quilt Applique Templates

Top of Iris
(Right Side)

Connect corresponding letters
and notches along dotted lines
and tape.

Completed layout will look
like this:

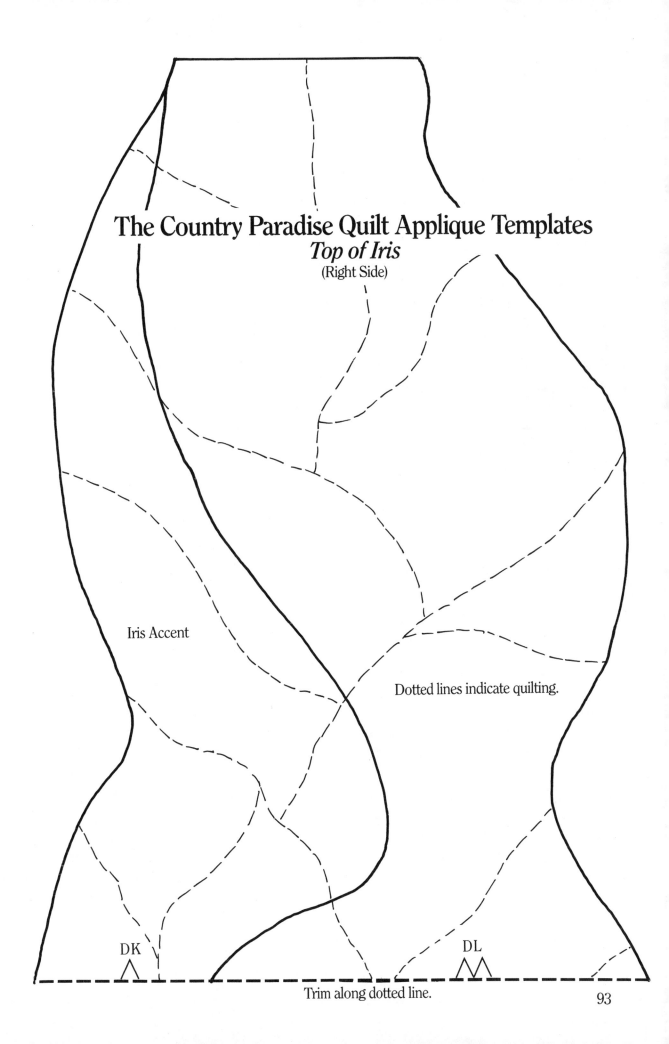

The Country Paradise Quilt Applique Templates
Top of Iris
(Right Side)

Iris Accent

Dotted lines indicate quilting.

DK

DL

Trim along dotted line.

The Country Paradise Quilt Applique Templates
Top of Iris
(Left Side)

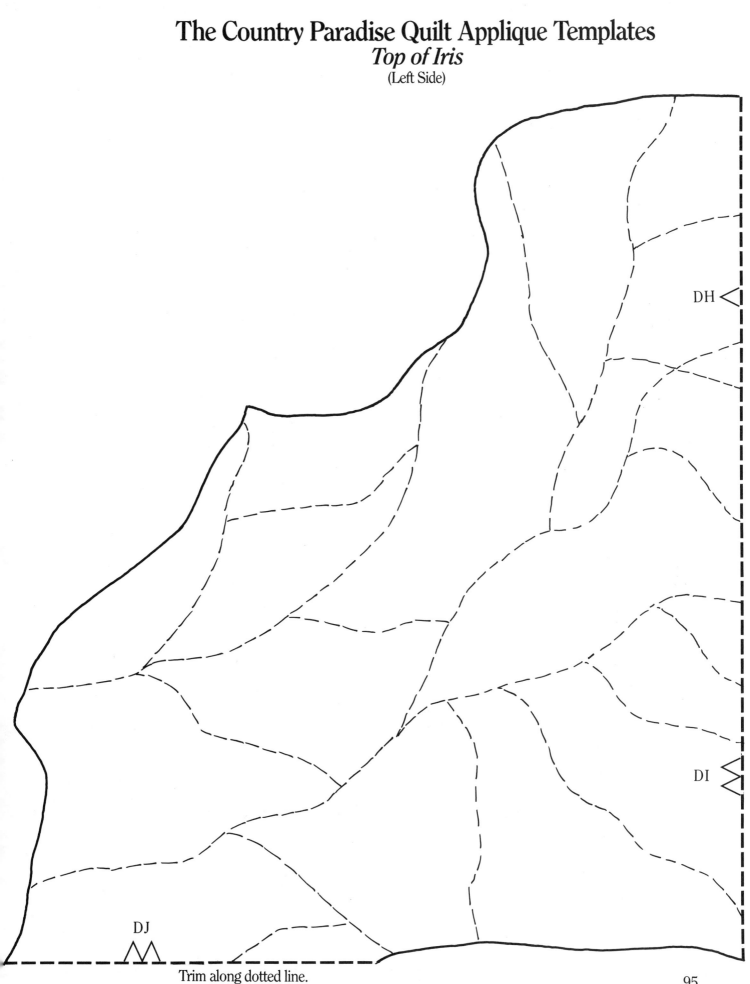

DH

DI

DJ

Trim along dotted line.

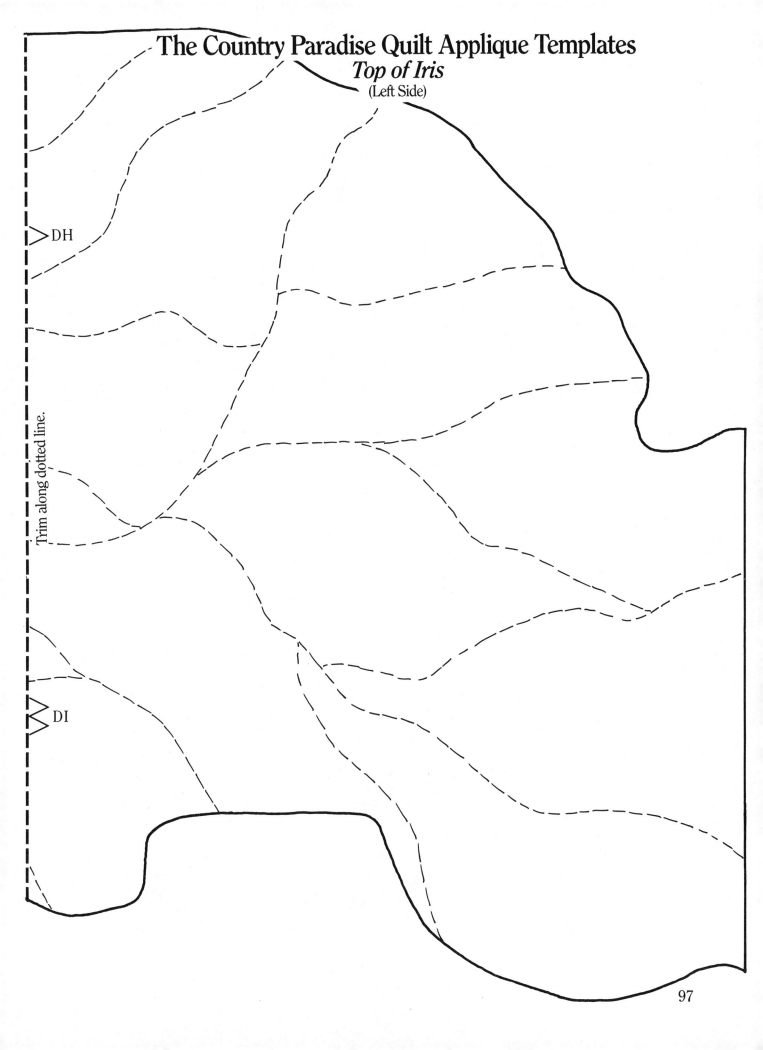

The Country Paradise Quilt Applique Templates
Top of Iris
(Left Side)

>DH

Trim along dotted line.

>DI

The Country Paradise Quilt Applique Templates
Iris

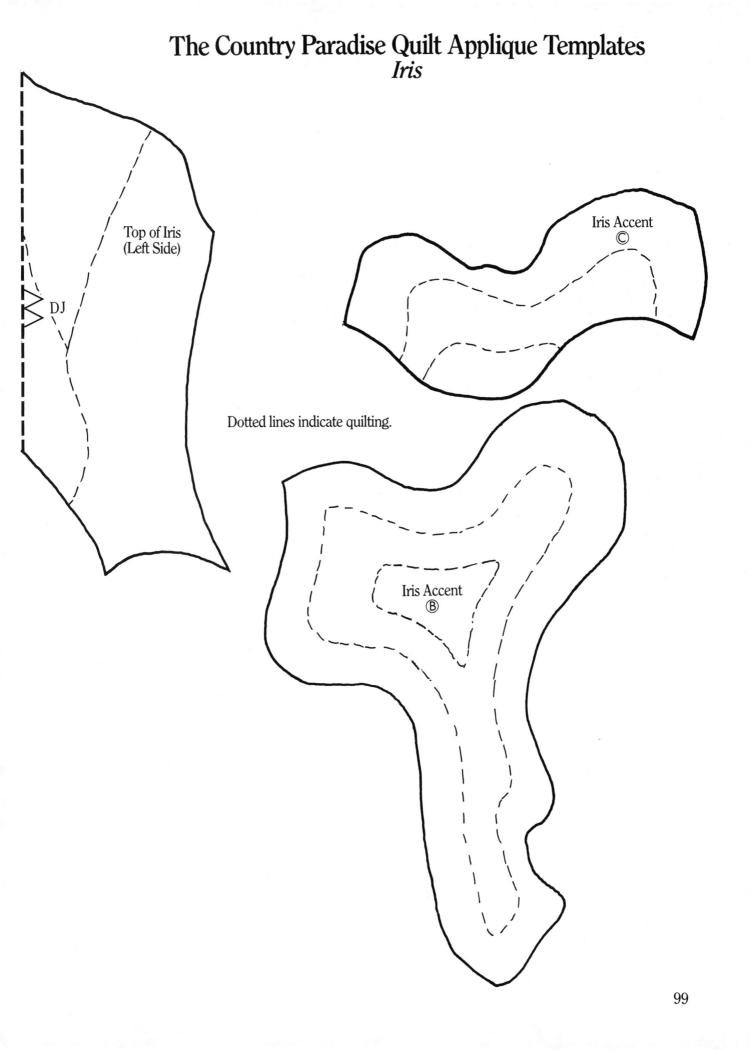

Top of Iris
(Left Side)

DJ

Iris Accent
©

Iris Accent
Ⓑ

Dotted lines indicate quilting.

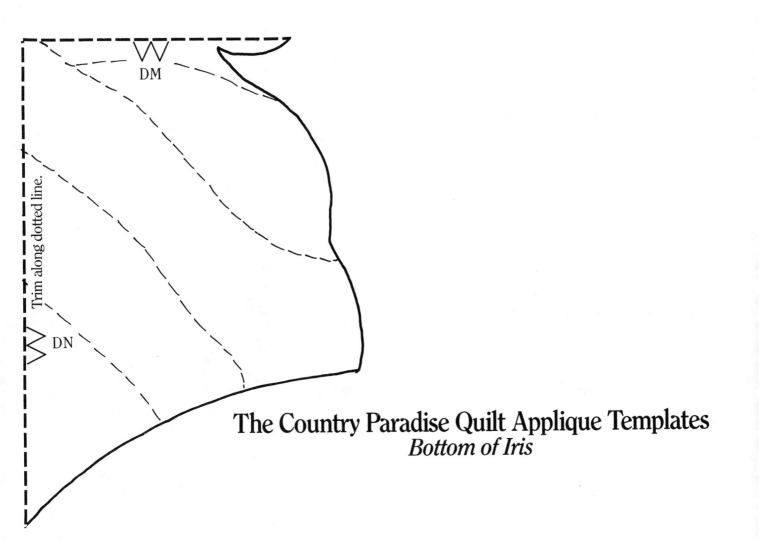

Trim along dotted line.

DM

DN

The Country Paradise Quilt Applique Templates
Bottom of Iris

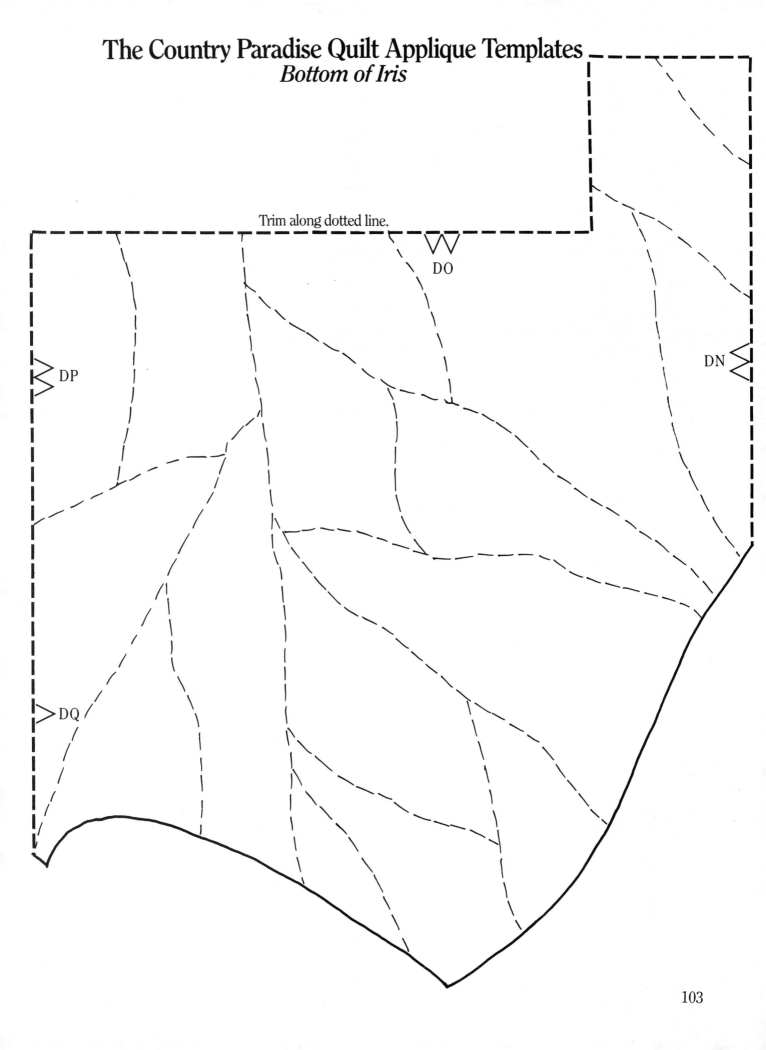

The Country Paradise Quilt Applique Templates
Bottom of Iris

Trim along dotted line.

DO

DP

DN

DQ

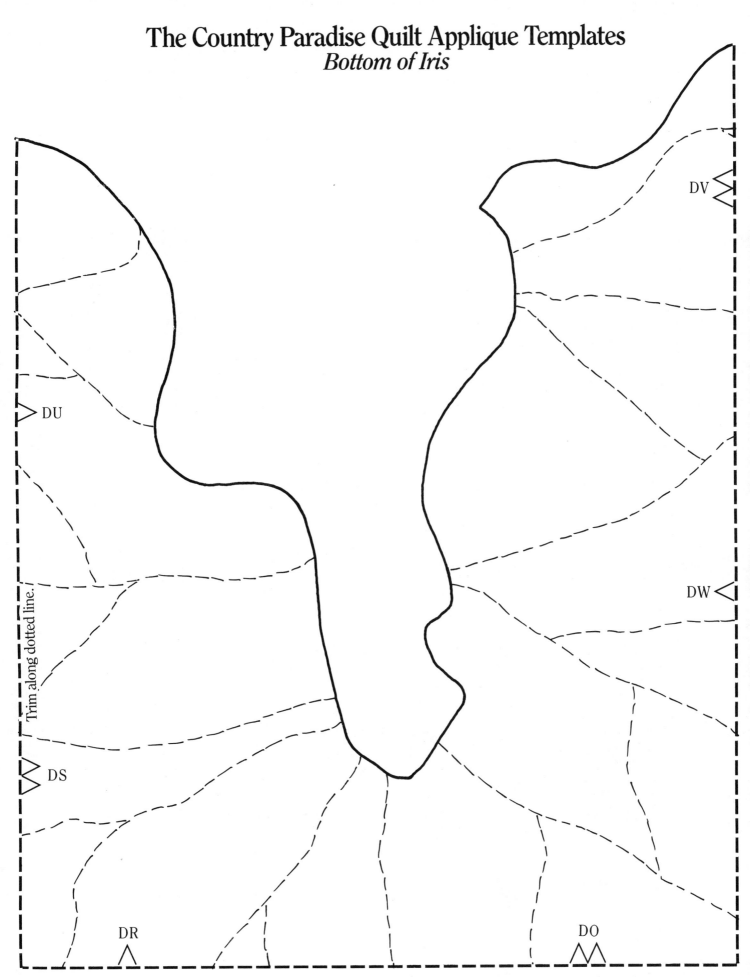

DV

DU

Trim along dotted line.

DW

DS

DR

DO

Bottom of Iris

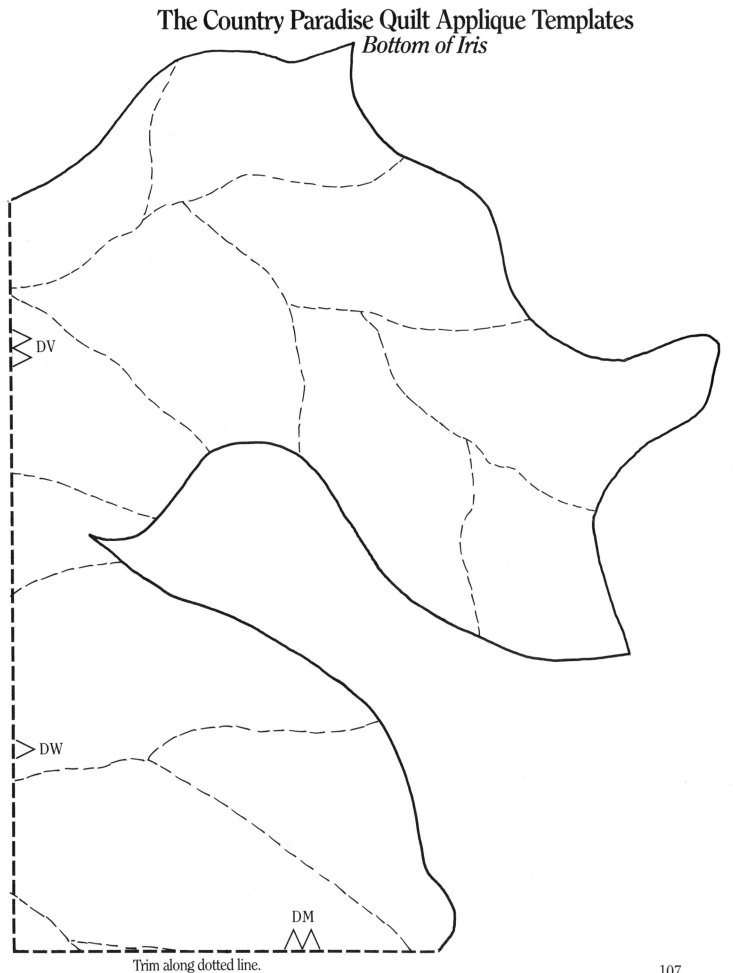

DV

DW

DM

Trim along dotted line.

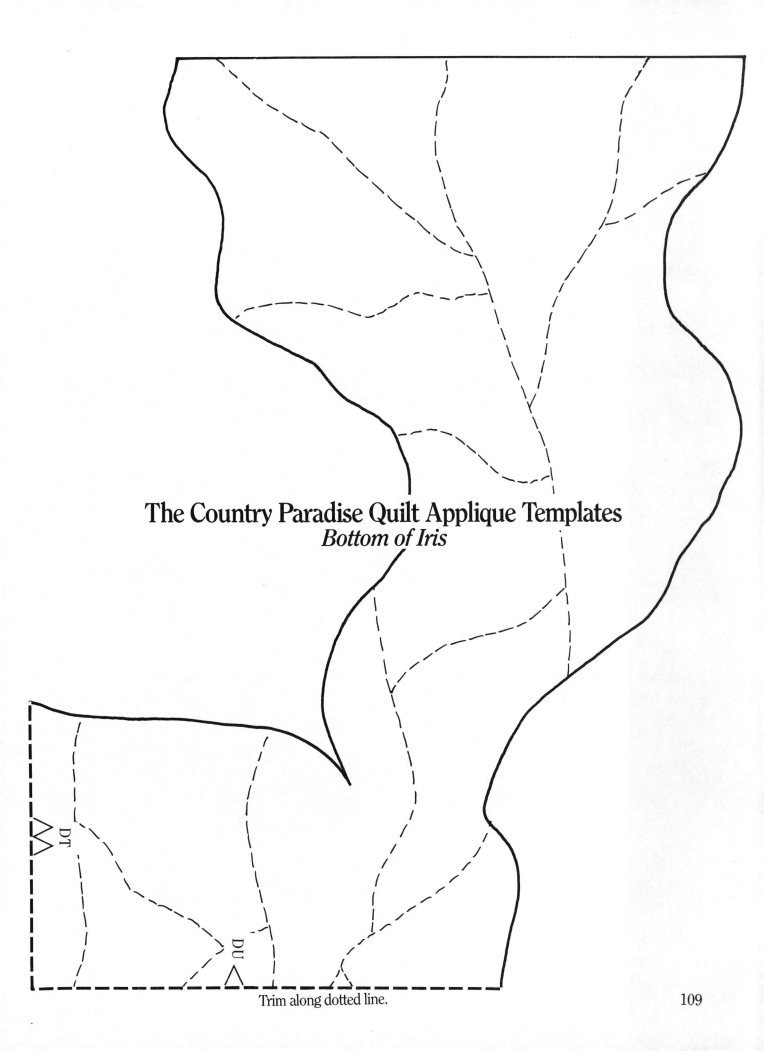

The Country Paradise Quilt Applique Templates
Bottom of Iris

DT

DU

Trim along dotted line.

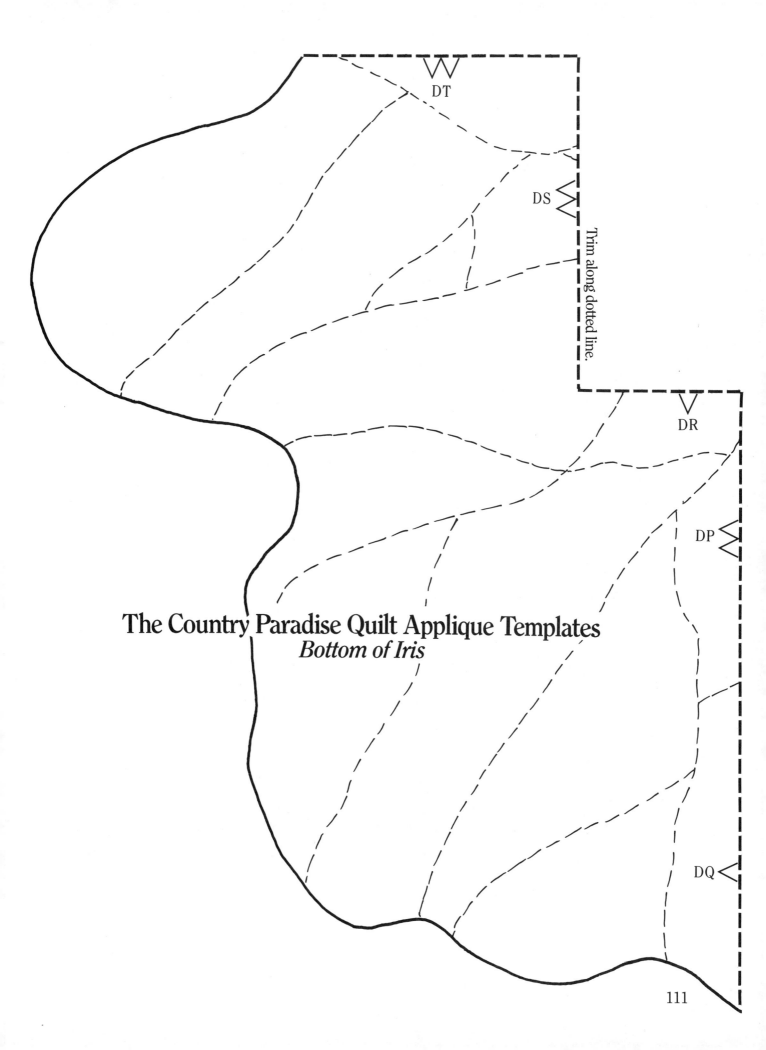

DT

DS

Trim along dotted line.

DR

DP

The Country Paradise Quilt Applique Templates
Bottom of Iris

DQ

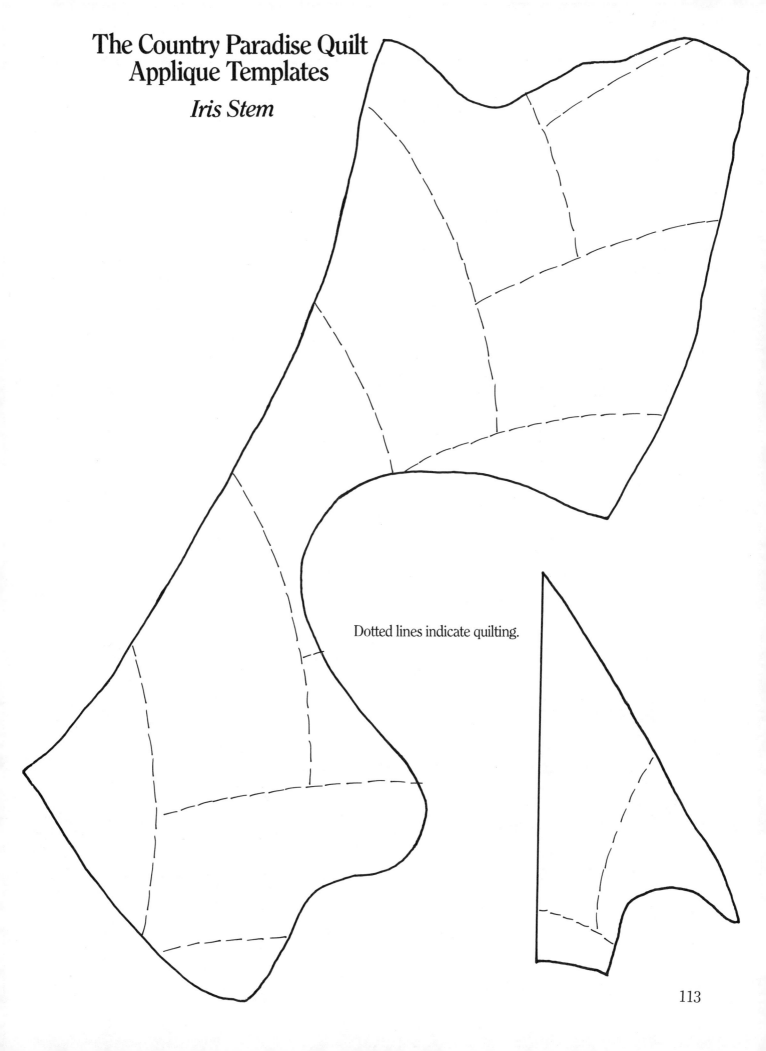

The Country Paradise Quilt
Applique Templates
Iris Stem

Dotted lines indicate quilting.

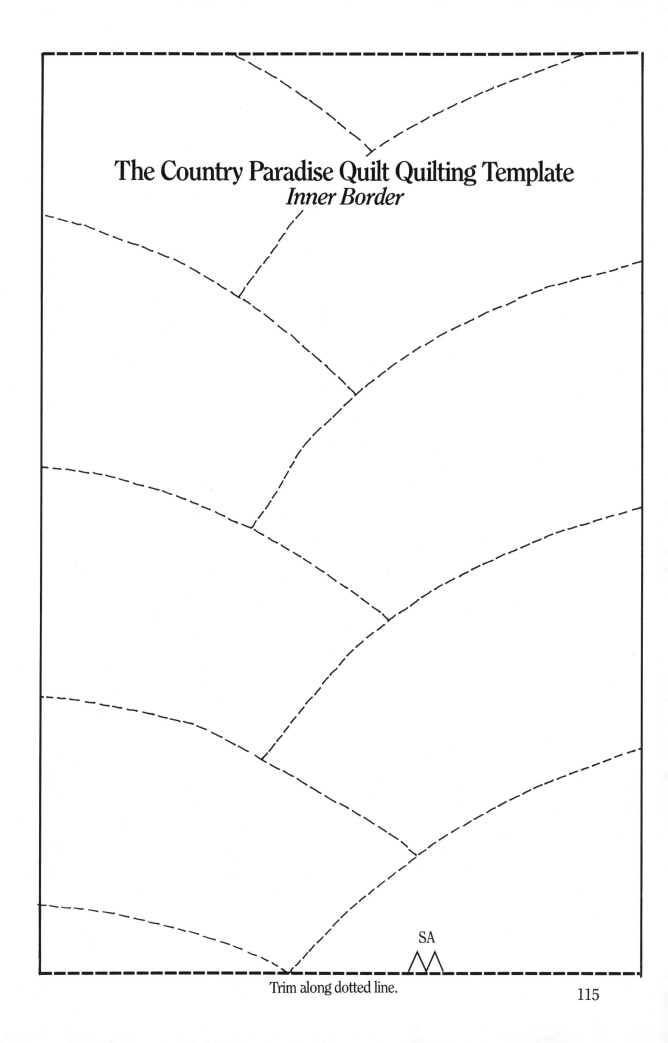

The Country Paradise Quilt Quilting Template
Inner Border

SA

Trim along dotted line.

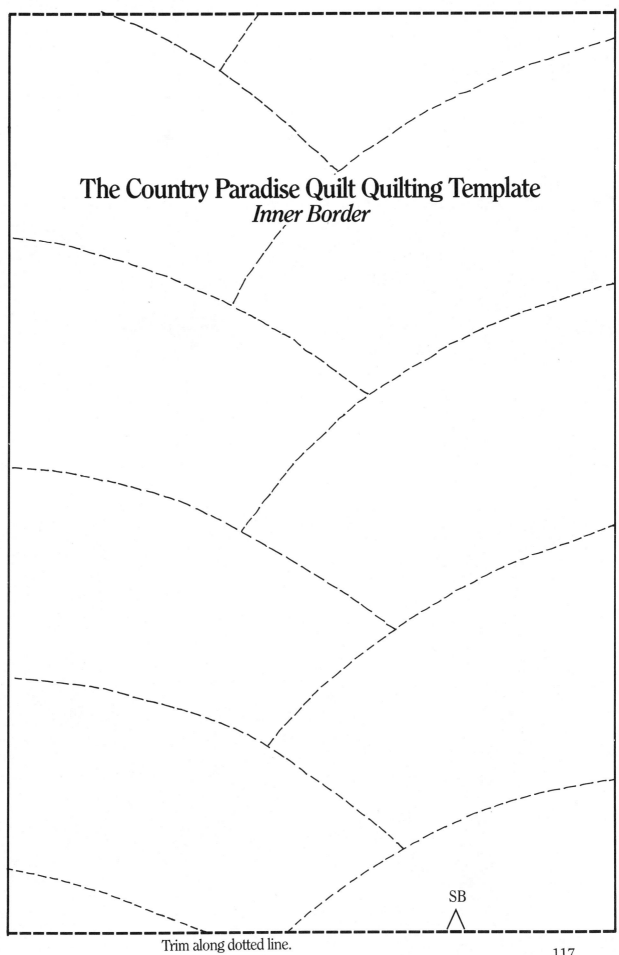

The Country Paradise Quilt Quilting Template
Inner Border

SB

Trim along dotted line.

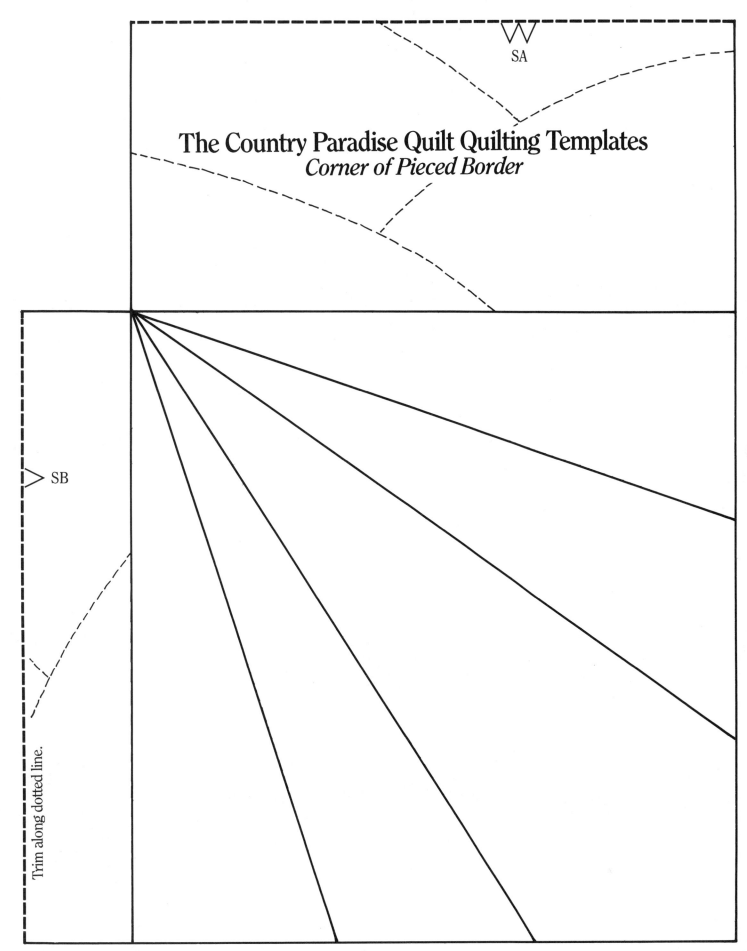

The Country Paradise Quilt Quilting Templates
Corner of Pieced Border

SA

SB

Trim along dotted line.

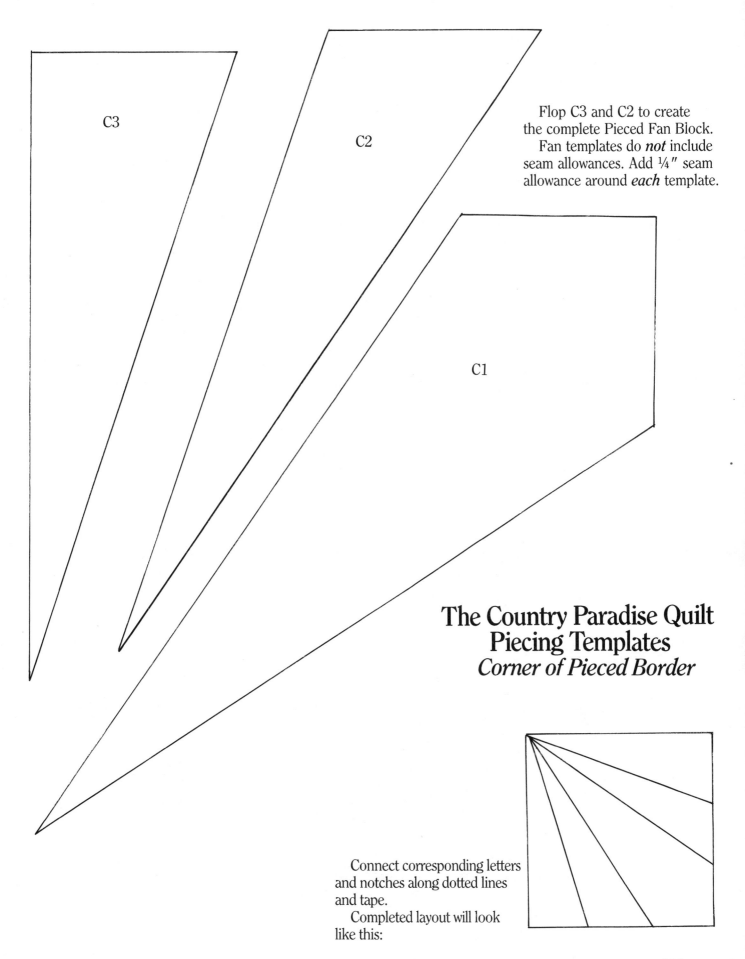

C3

C2

Flop C3 and C2 to create the complete Pieced Fan Block. Fan templates do *not* include seam allowances. Add ¼" seam allowance around *each* template.

C1

The Country Paradise Quilt
Piecing Templates
Corner of Pieced Border

Connect corresponding letters and notches along dotted lines and tape.

Completed layout will look like this:

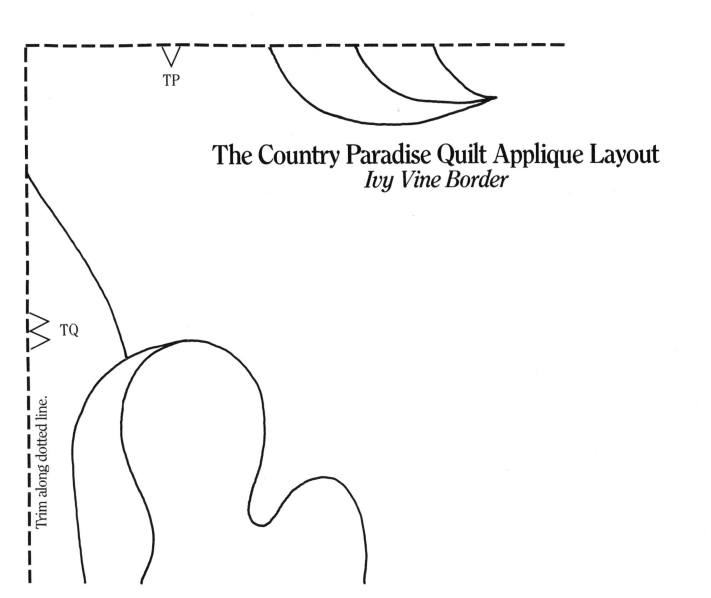

The Country Paradise Quilt Applique Layout
Ivy Vine Border

TP

TQ

Trim along dotted line.

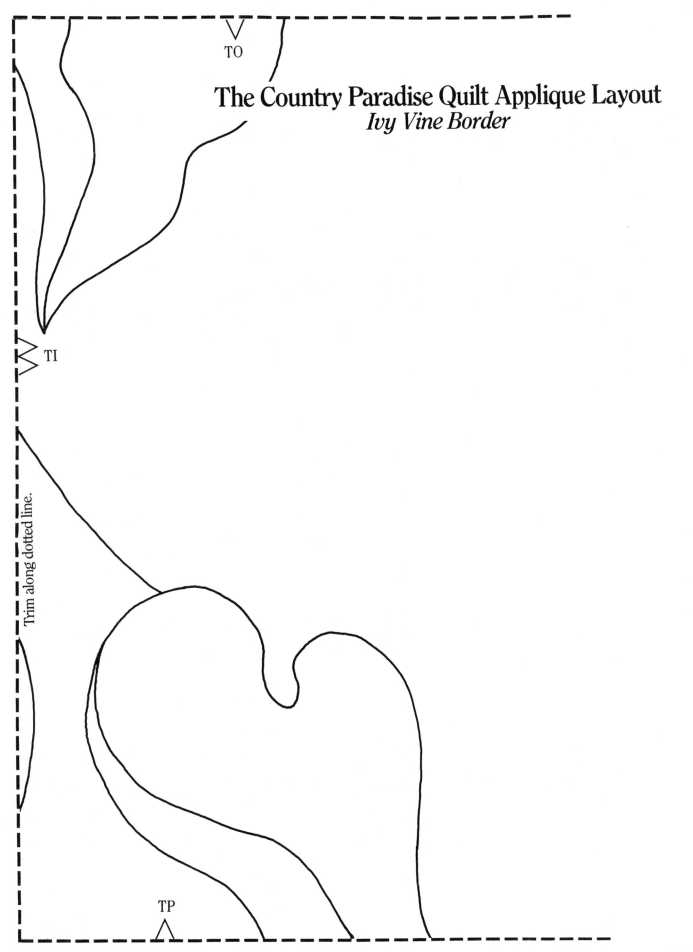

The Country Paradise Quilt Applique Layout
Ivy Vine Border

TO

TI

Trim along dotted line.

TP

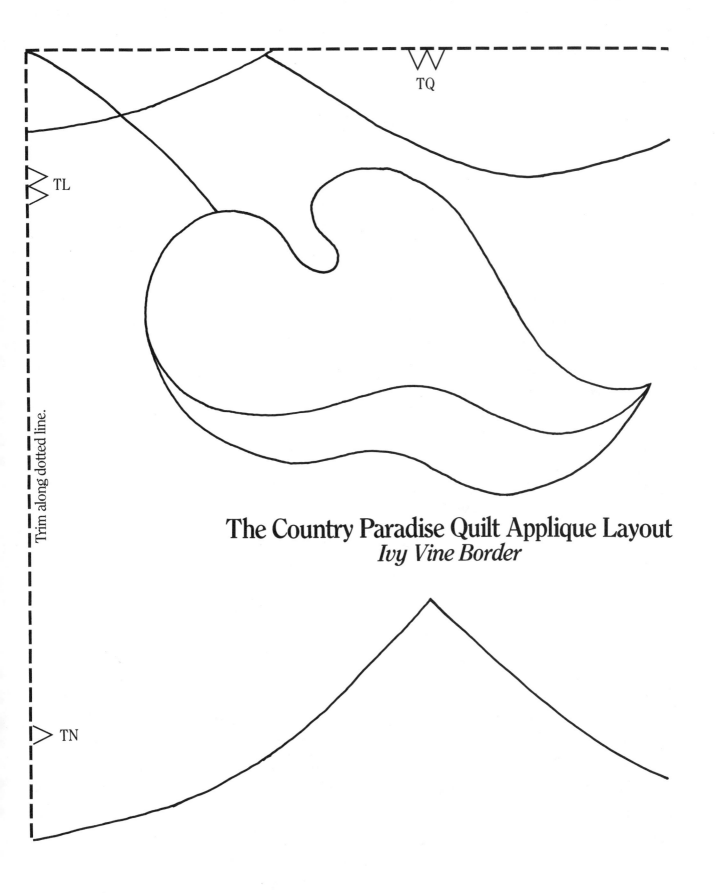

Trim along dotted line.

TQ

TL

TN

The Country Paradise Quilt Applique Layout
Ivy Vine Border

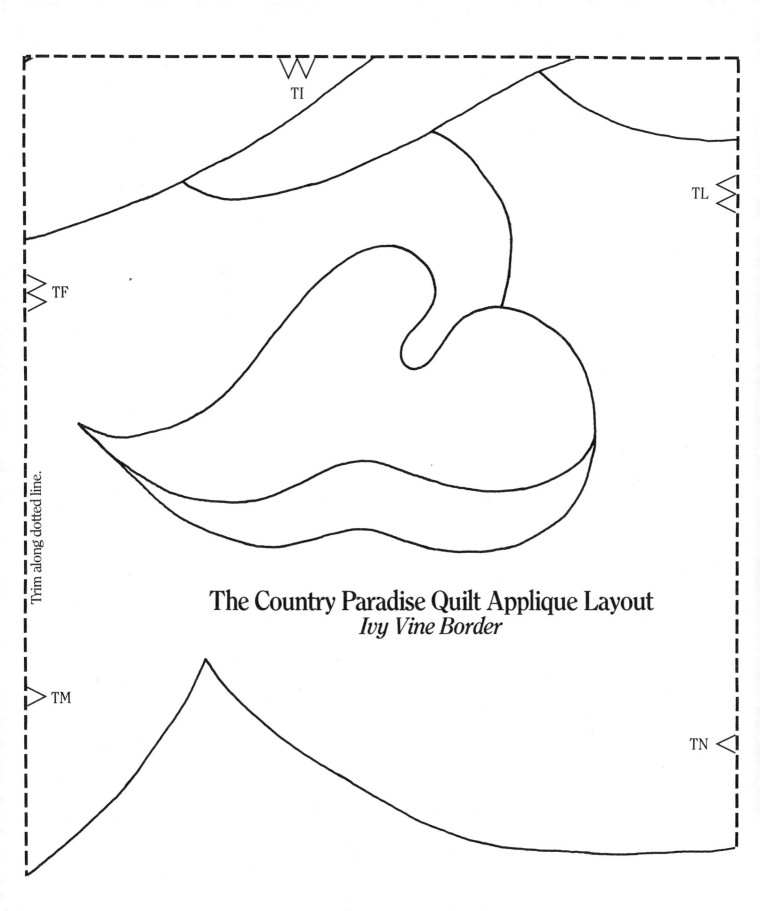

TI

TL

TF

TM

The Country Paradise Quilt Applique Layout
Ivy Vine Border

TN

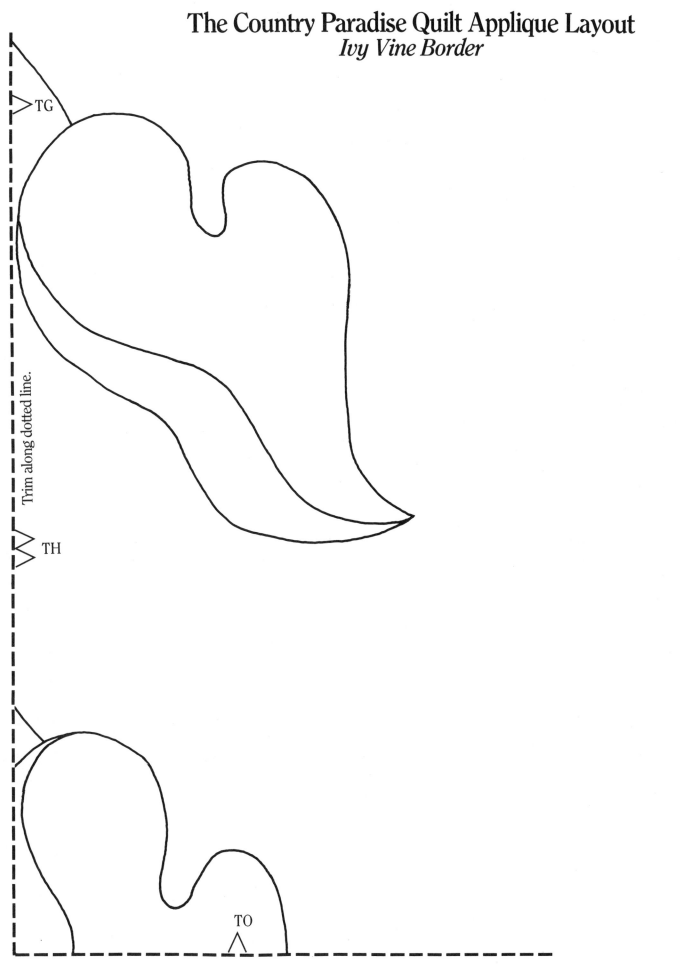

TG

Trim along dotted line.

TH

TO

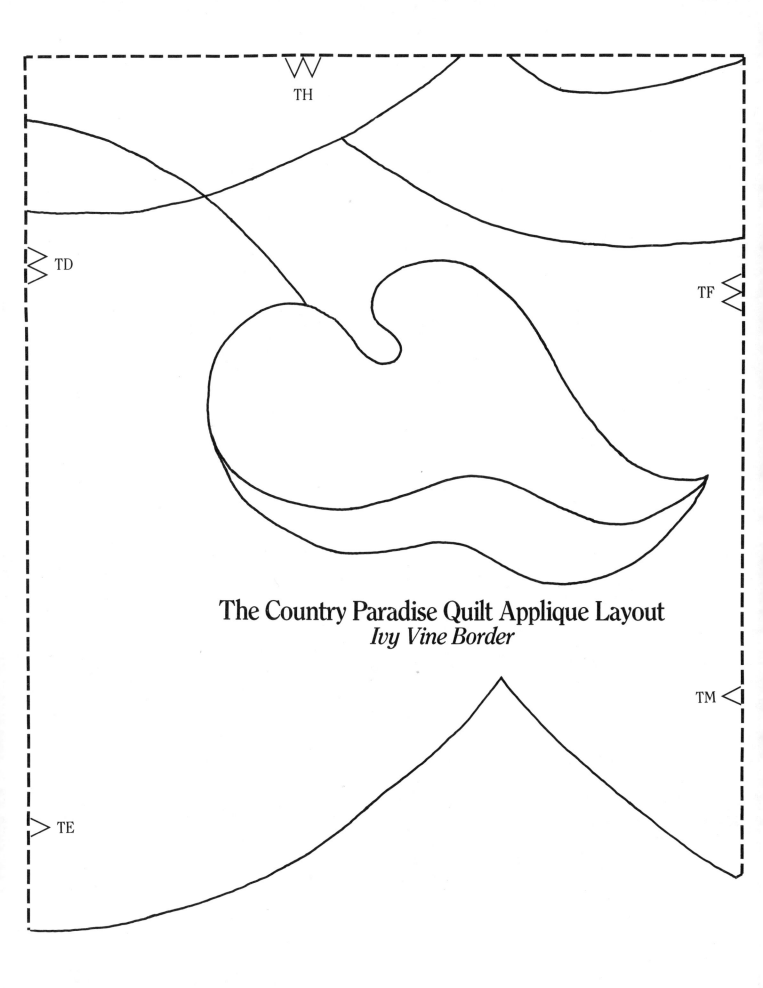

The Country Paradise Quilt Applique Layout
Ivy Vine Border

TH

TD

TF

TM

TE

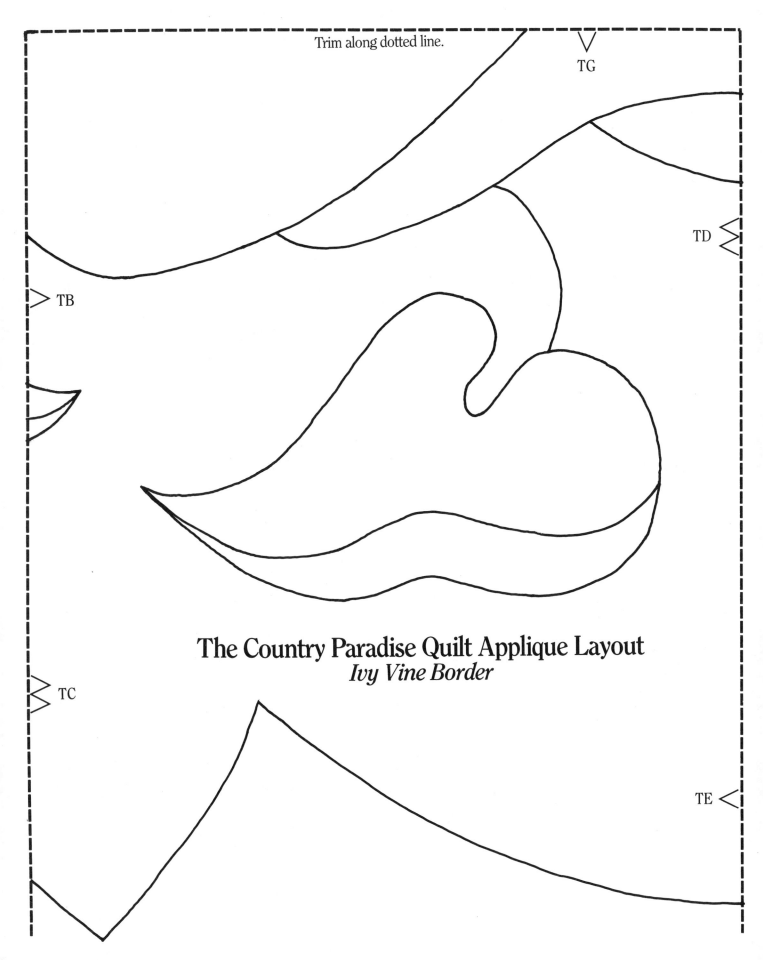

Trim along dotted line.

TG

TD

TB

TC

The Country Paradise Quilt Applique Layout
Ivy Vine Border

TE

135

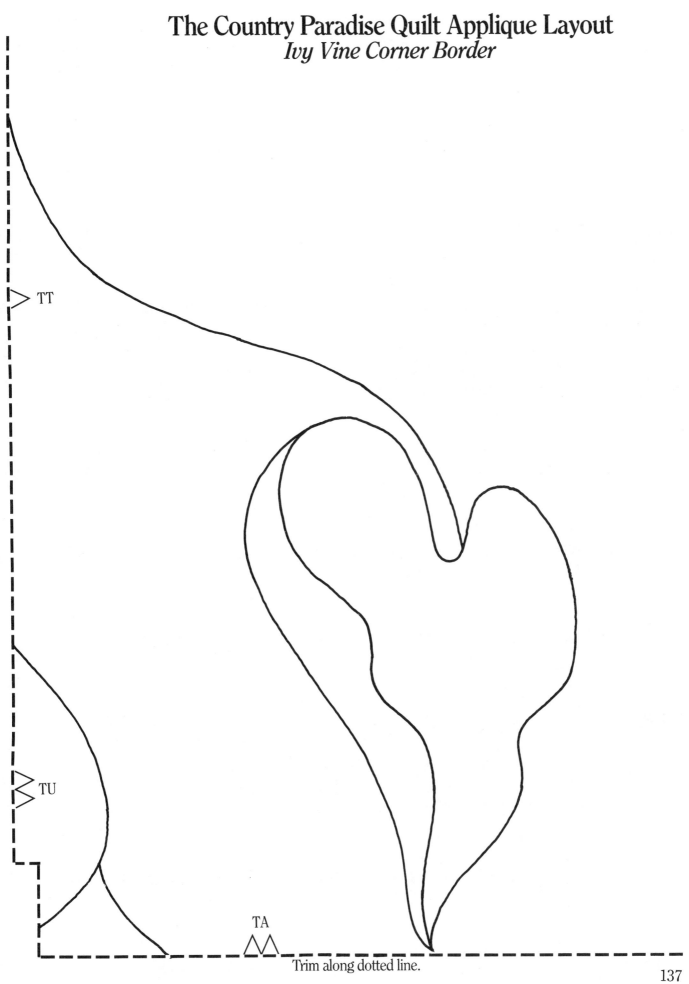

The Country Paradise Quilt Applique Layout
Ivy Vine Corner Border

TT

TU

TA

Trim along dotted line.

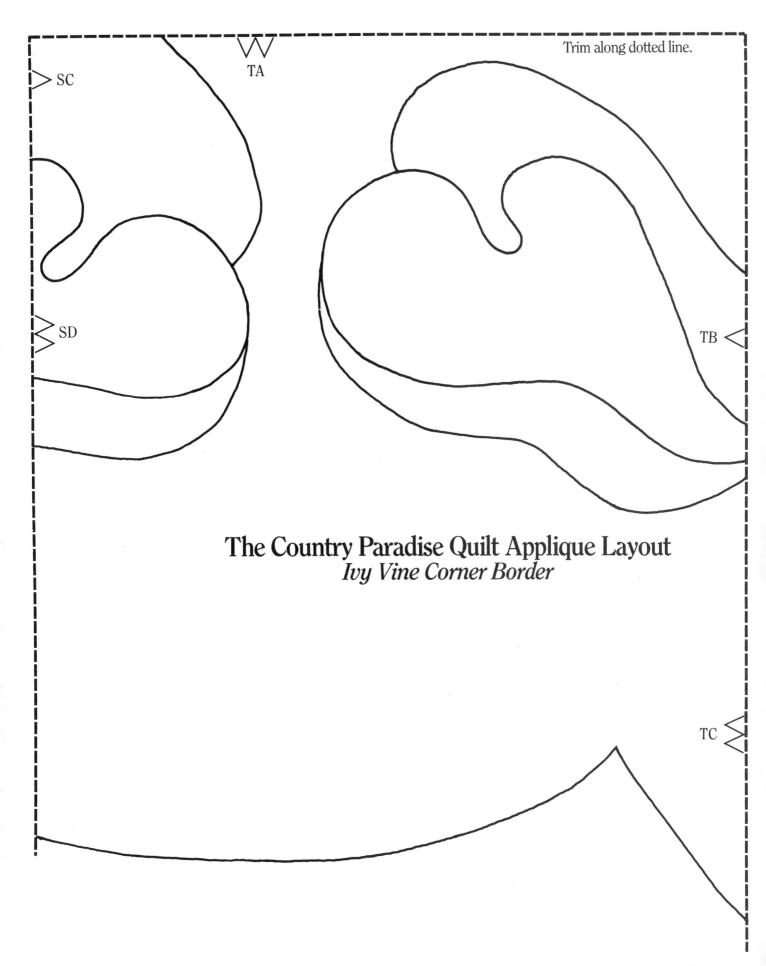

SC

TA

SD

TB

The Country Paradise Quilt Applique Layout
Ivy Vine Corner Border

TC

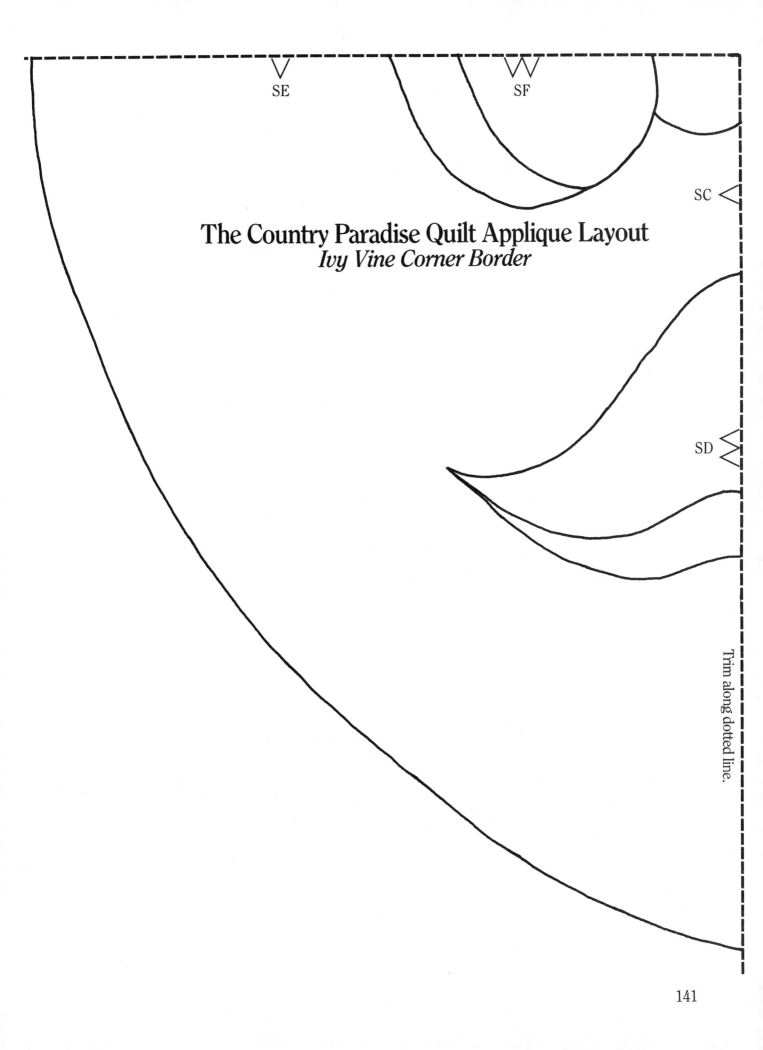

The Country Paradise Quilt Applique Layout
Ivy Vine Corner Border

SE

SF

SC

SD

Trim along dotted line.

141

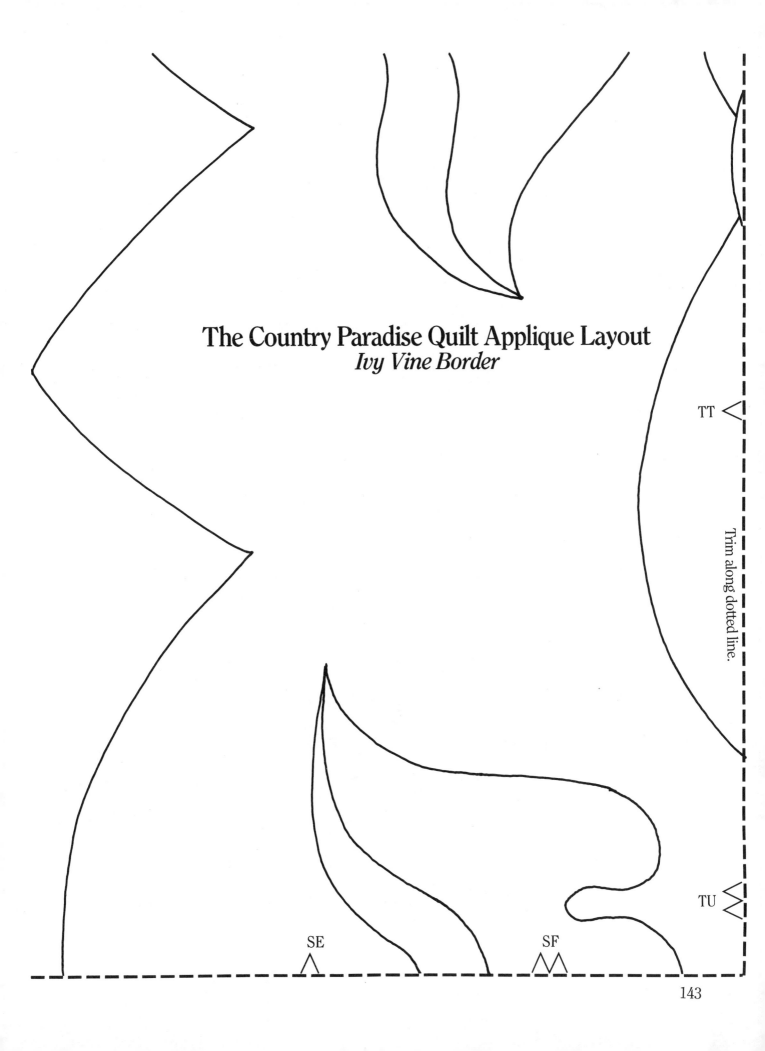

The Country Paradise Quilt Applique Layout
Ivy Vine Border

TT

Trim along dotted line.

TU

SE

SF

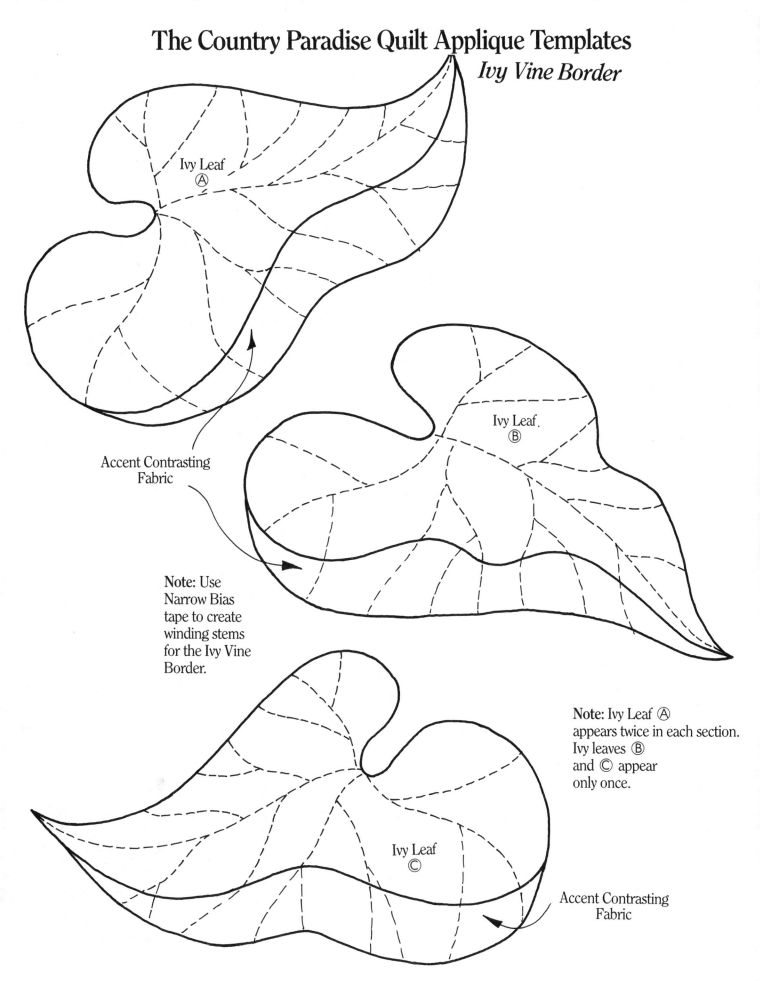

Ivy Leaf
Ⓐ

Ivy Leaf
Ⓑ

Ivy Leaf
Ⓒ

Accent Contrasting
Fabric

Note: Use
Narrow Bias
tape to create
winding stems
for the Ivy Vine
Border.

Note: Ivy Leaf Ⓐ
appears twice in each section.
Ivy leaves Ⓑ
and Ⓒ appear
only once.

Accent Contrasting
Fabric

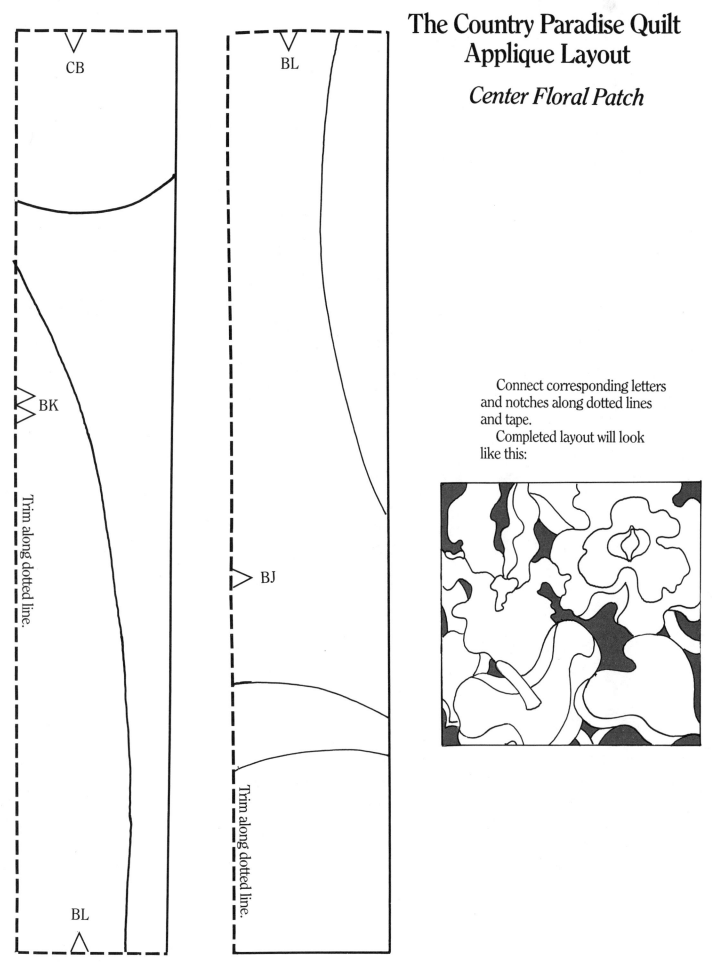

The Country Paradise Quilt
Applique Layout
Center Floral Patch

CB

BL

BK

Trim along dotted line.

BJ

BL

Trim along dotted line.

Connect corresponding letters
and notches along dotted lines
and tape.

Completed layout will look
like this:

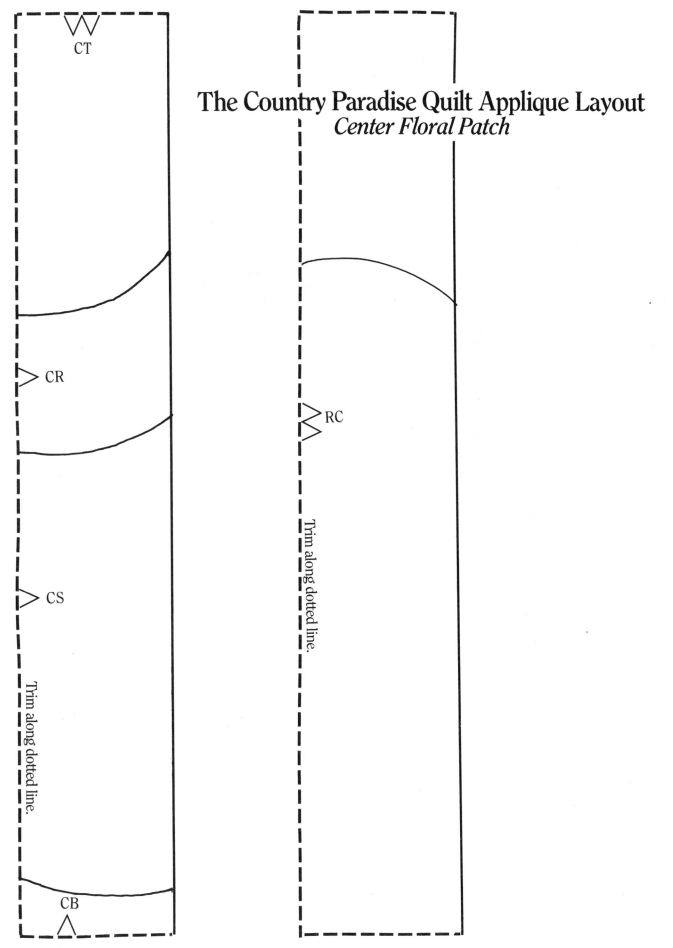

The Country Paradise Quilt Applique Layout
Center Floral Patch

CT

CR

CS

Trim along dotted line.

CB

RC

Trim along dotted line.

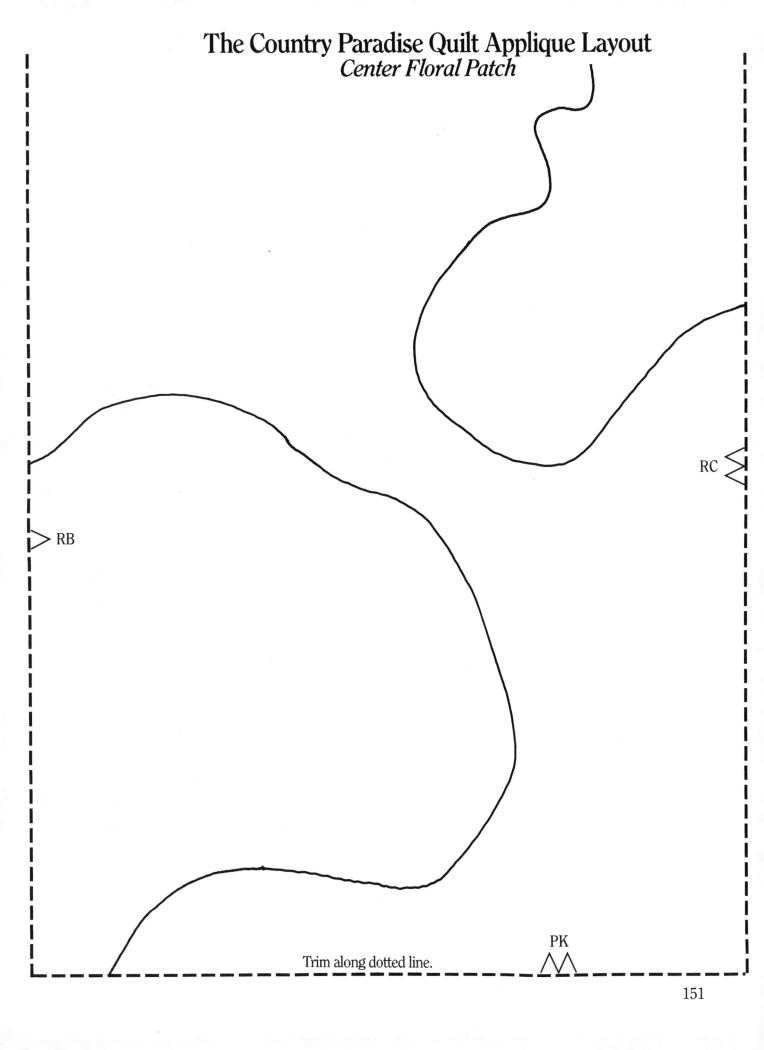

The Country Paradise Quilt Applique Layout
Center Floral Patch

RC

RB

PK

Trim along dotted line.

The Country Paradise Quilt Applique Layout
Center Floral Patch

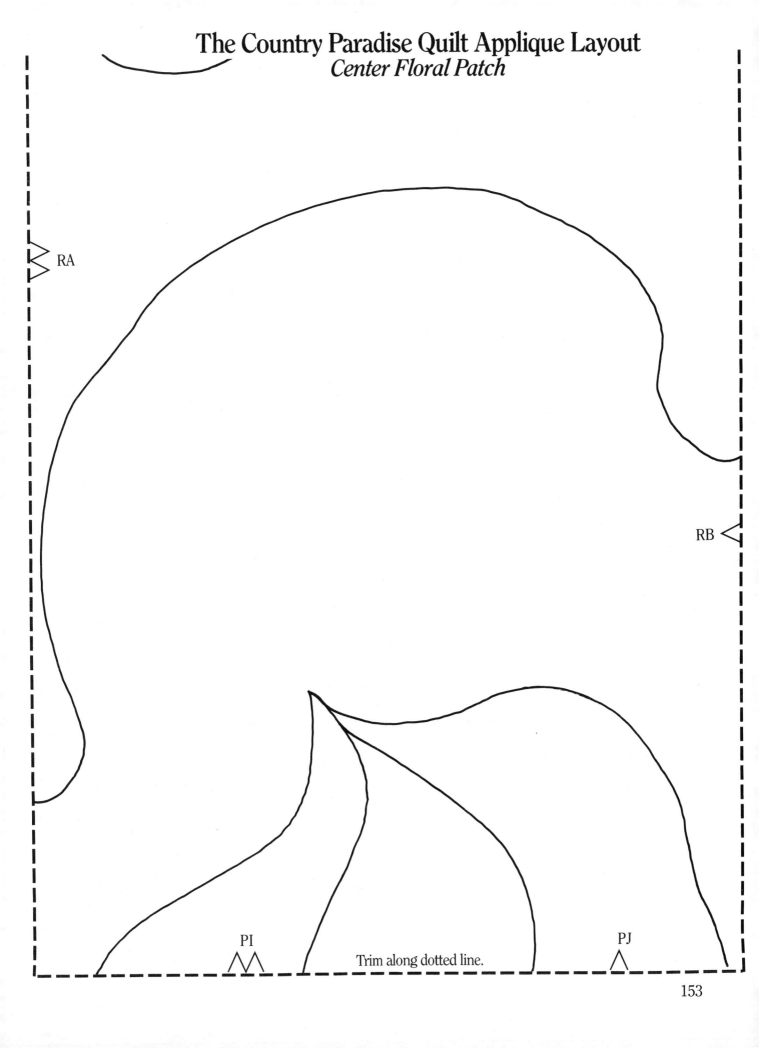

RA

RB

PI

PJ

Trim along dotted line.

The Country Paradise Quilt Applique Layout
Center Floral Patch

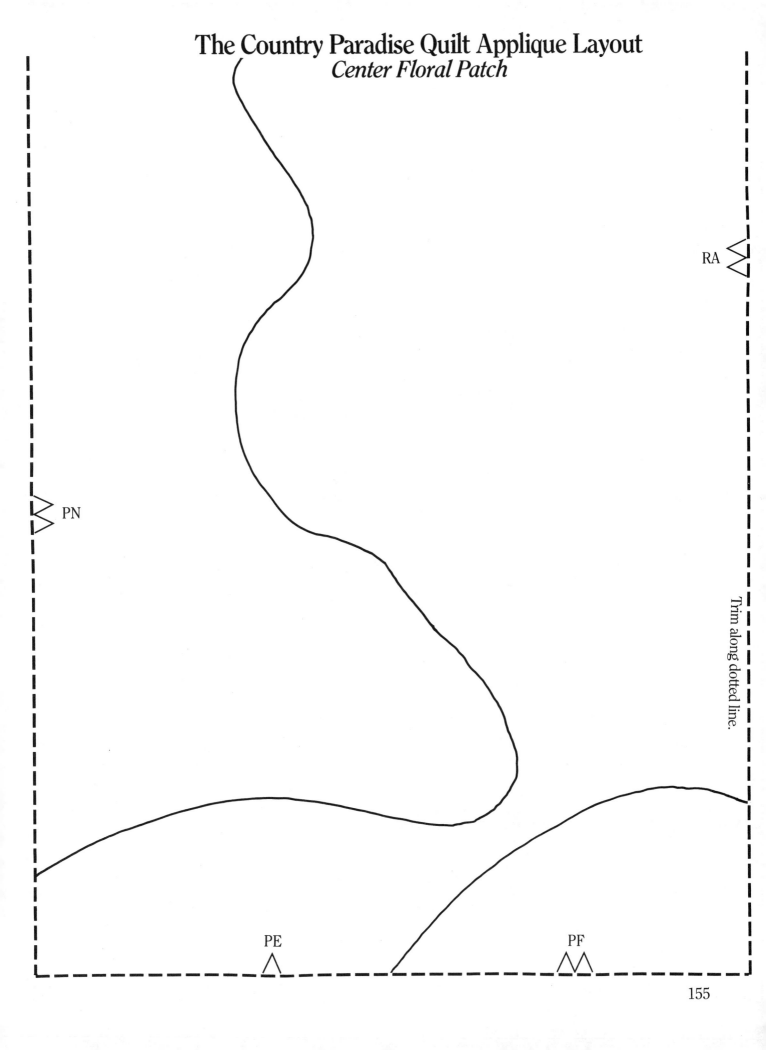

RA

PN

Trim along dotted line.

PE

PF

The Country Paradise Quilt Applique Layout
Center Floral Patch

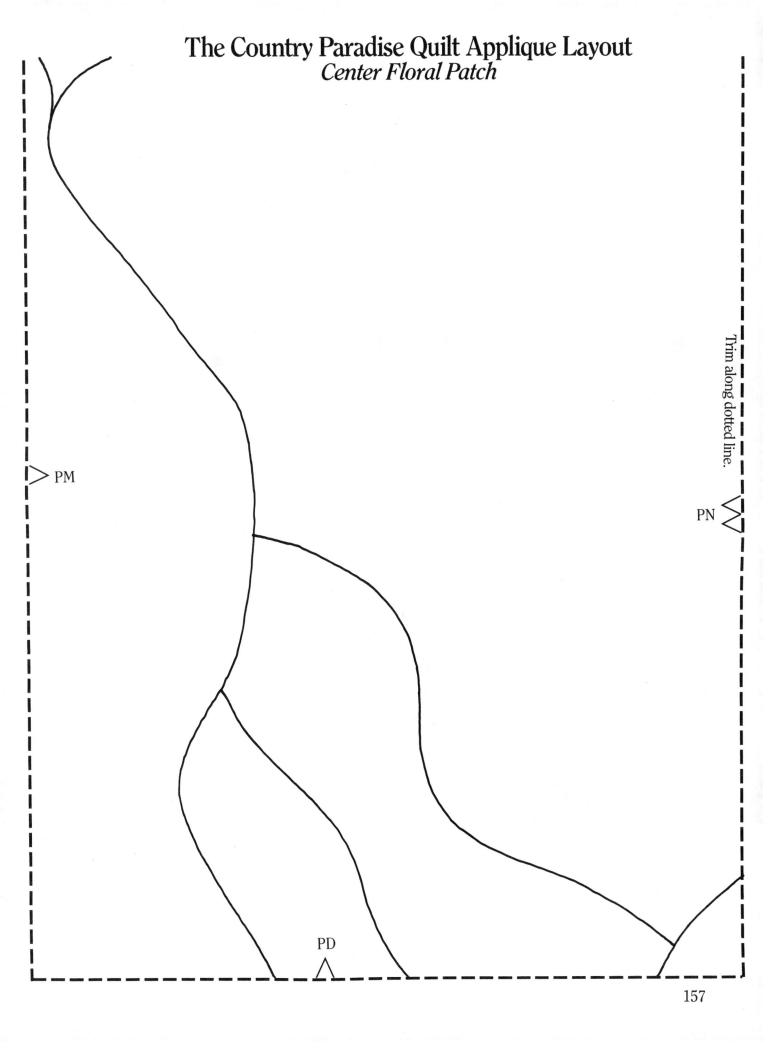

PM

PN

Trim along dotted line.

PD

The Country Paradise Quilt Applique Layout
Center Floral Patch

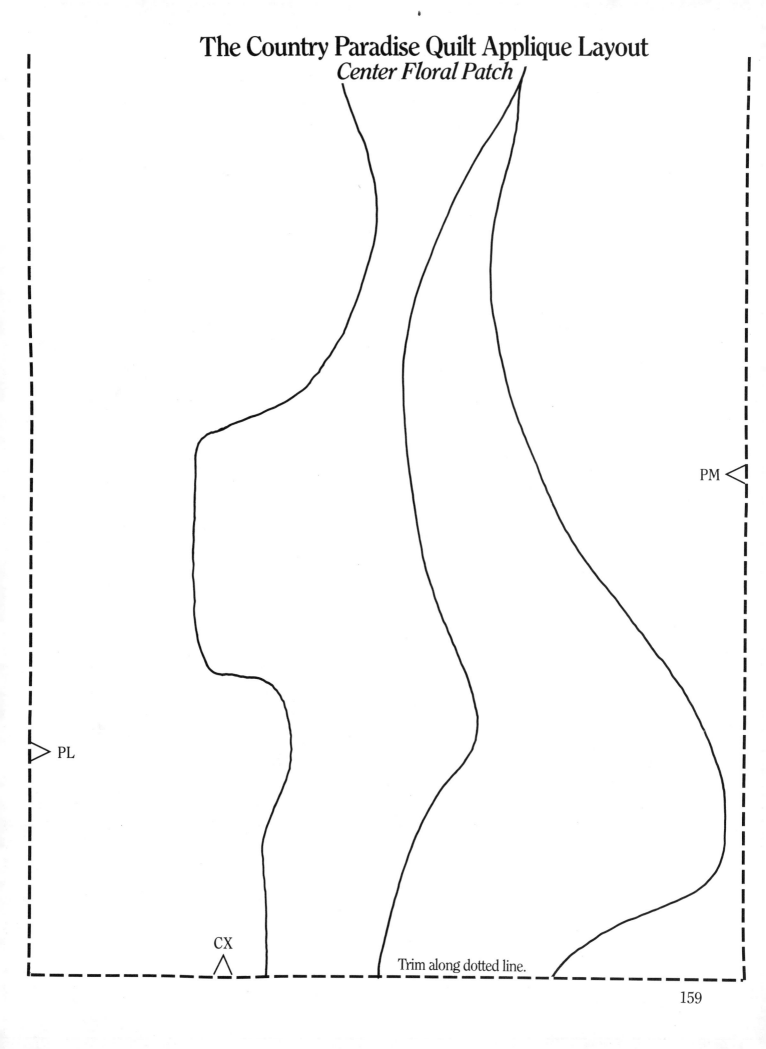

PM ◁

PL ▷

CX
△

Trim along dotted line.

The Country Paradise Quilt Applique Layout
Center Floral Patch

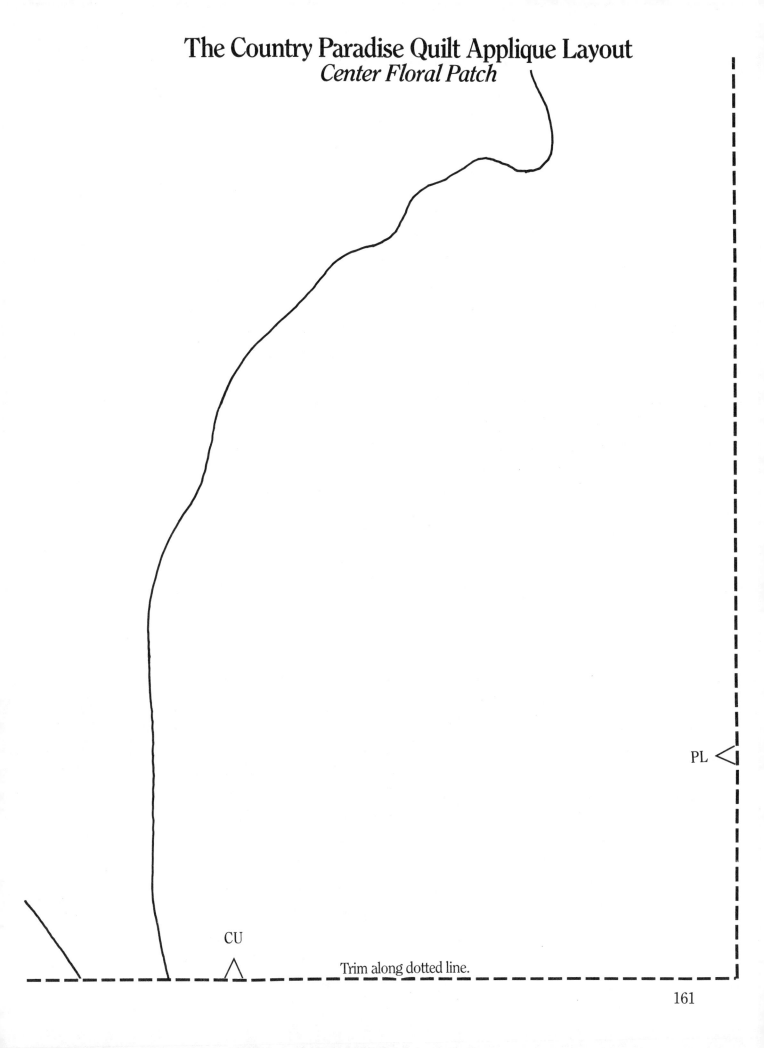

PL

CU

Trim along dotted line.

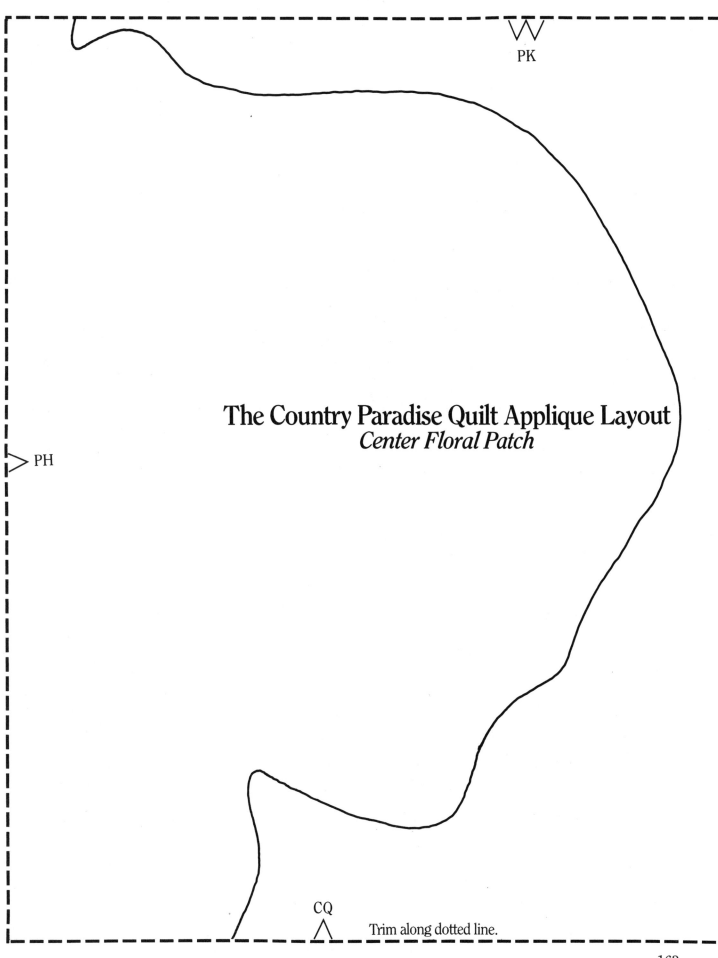

The Country Paradise Quilt Applique Layout
Center Floral Patch

PK

PH

CQ

Trim along dotted line.

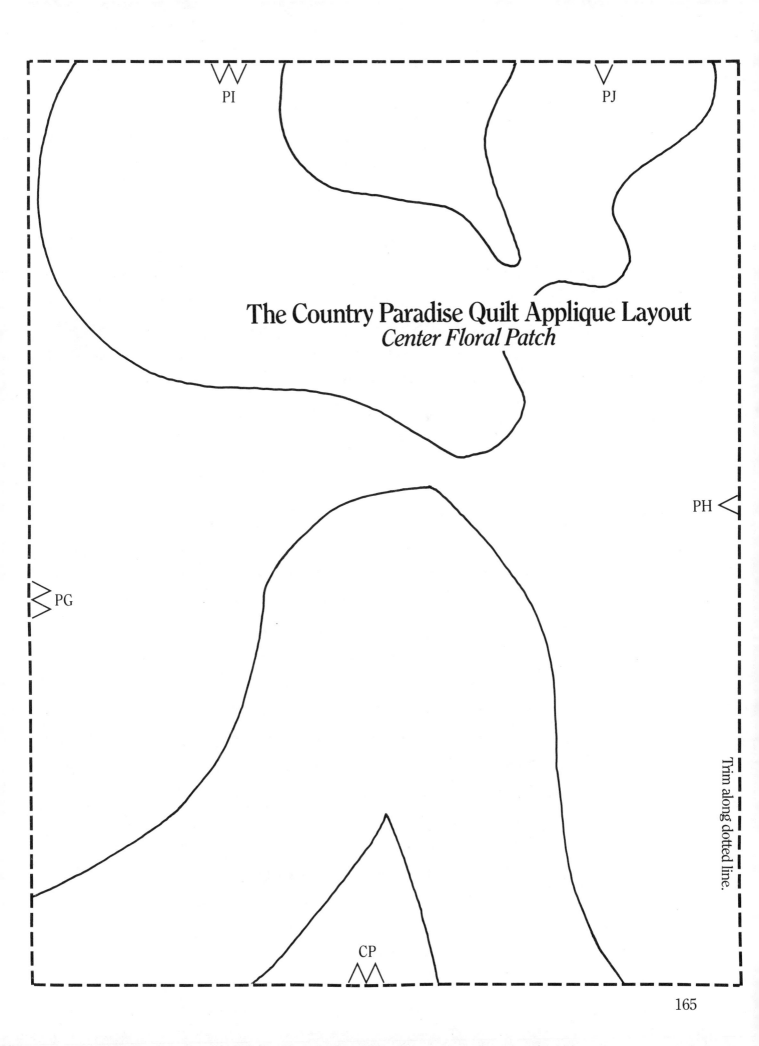

The Country Paradise Quilt Applique Layout
Center Floral Patch

PI

PJ

PH

PG

CP

Trim along dotted line.

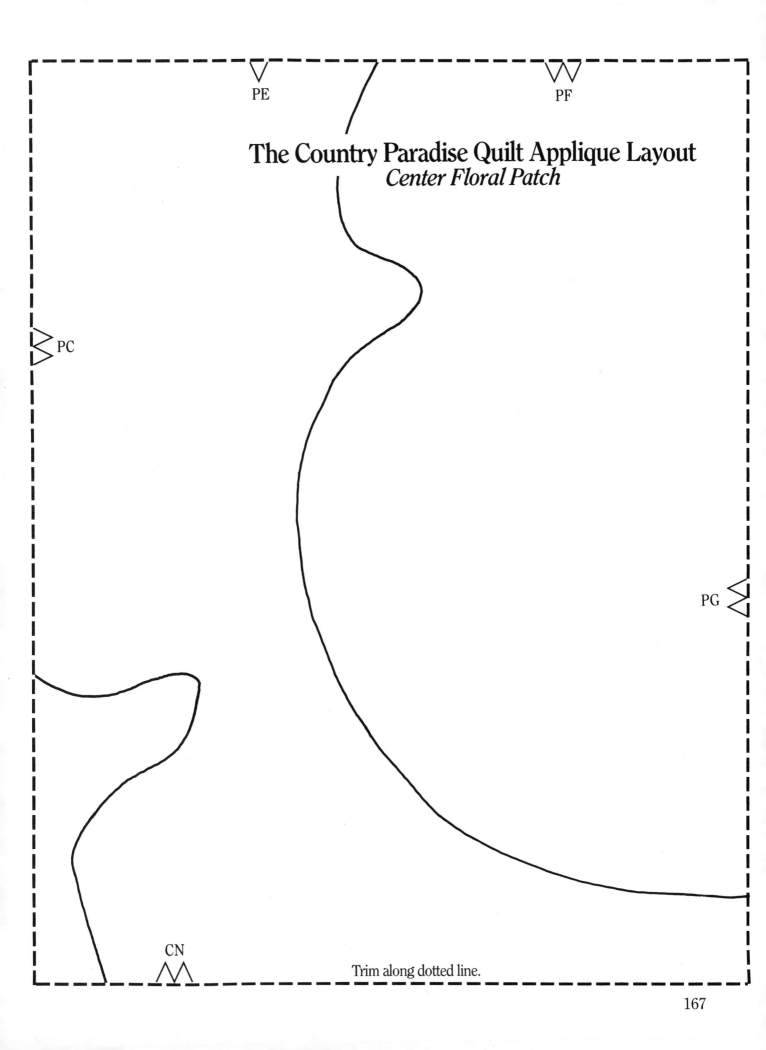

PE

PF

The Country Paradise Quilt Applique Layout
Center Floral Patch

PC

PG

CN

Trim along dotted line.

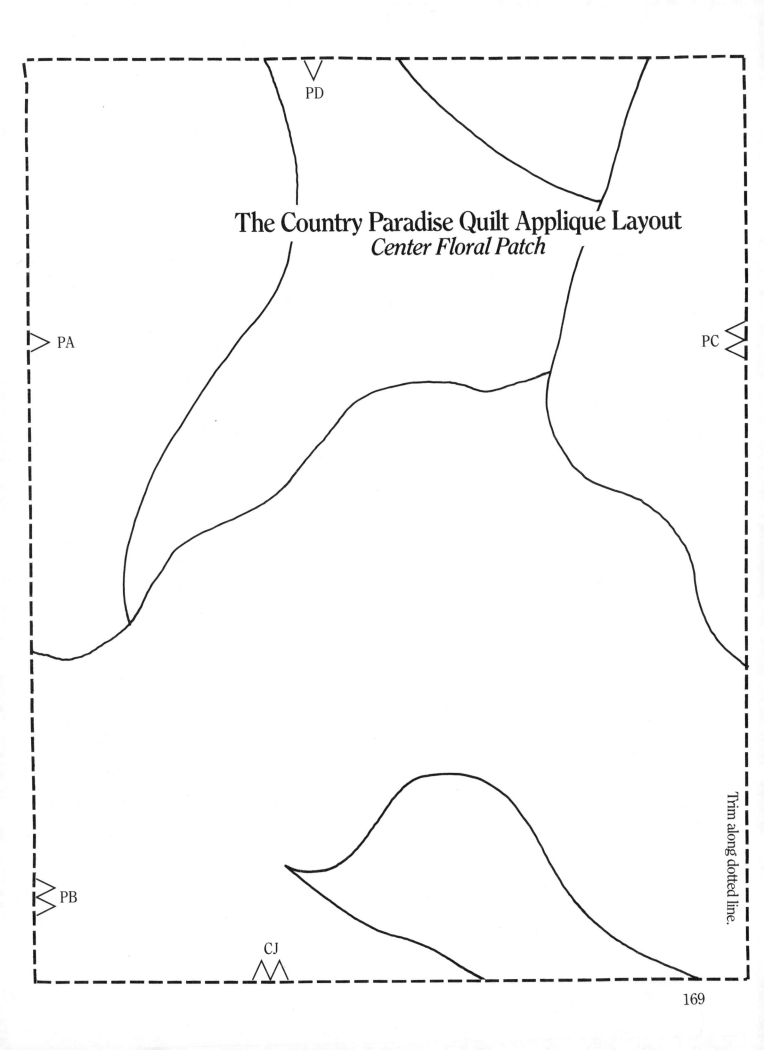

The Country Paradise Quilt Applique Layout
Center Floral Patch

PD

PA

PC

PB

CJ

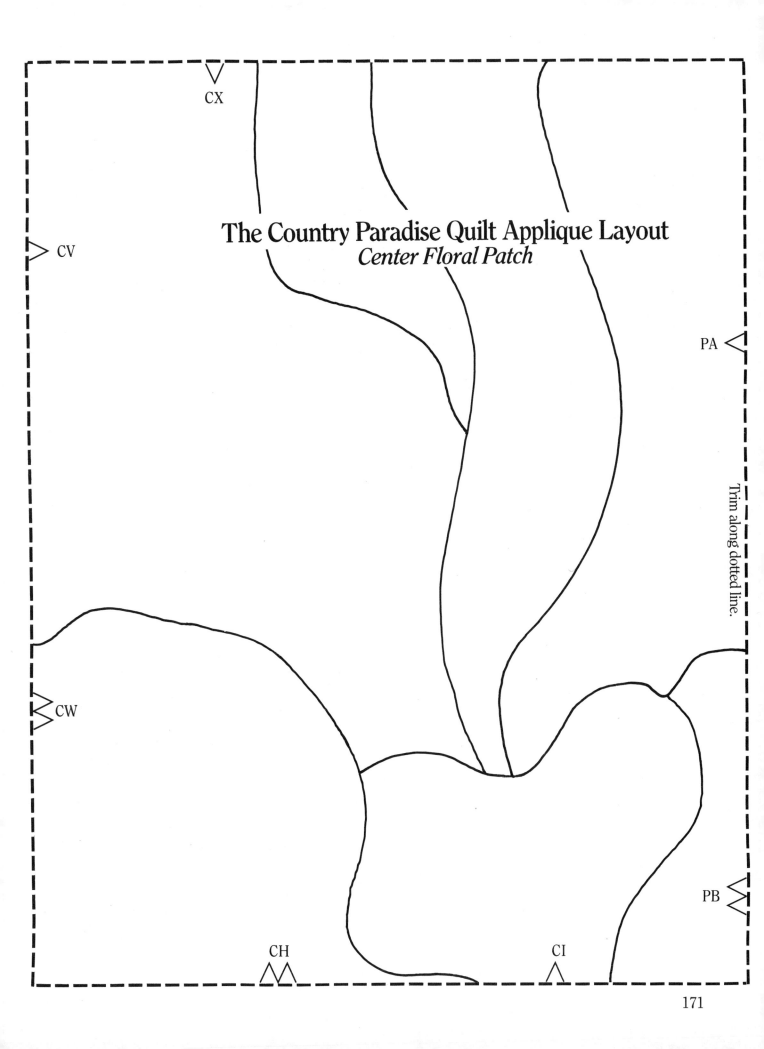

The Country Paradise Quilt Applique Layout
Center Floral Patch

CX

CV

PA

CW

CH

CI

PB

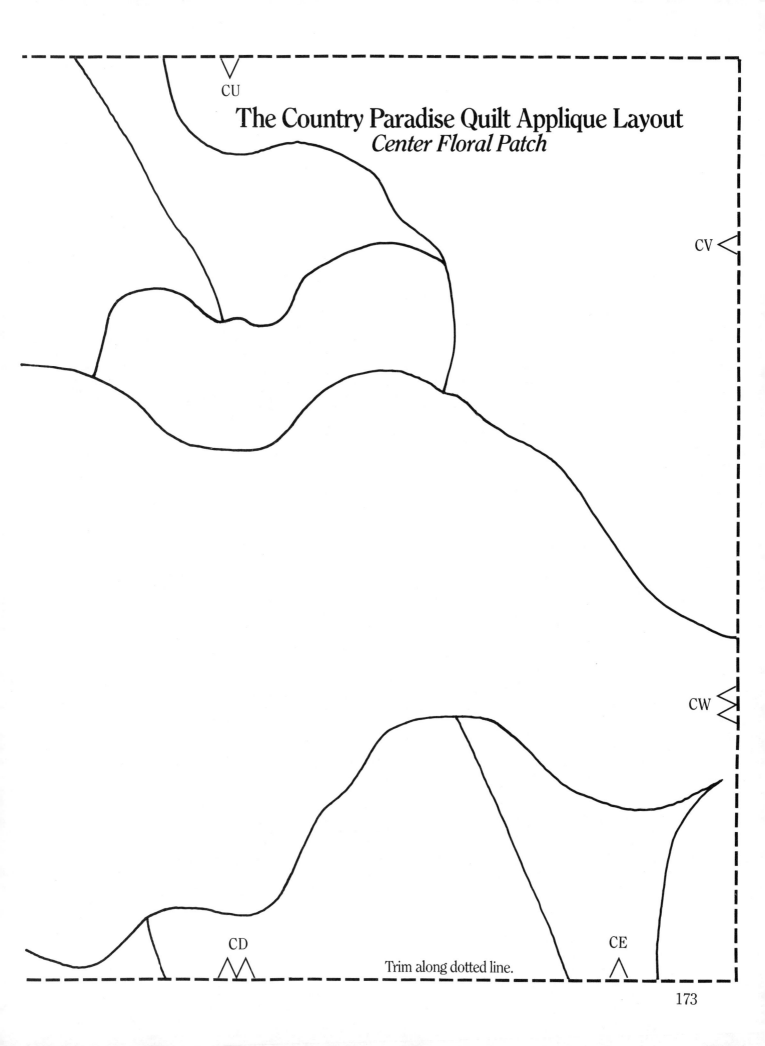

The Country Paradise Quilt Applique Layout
Center Floral Patch

CU

CV

CW

CD

CE

Trim along dotted line.

173

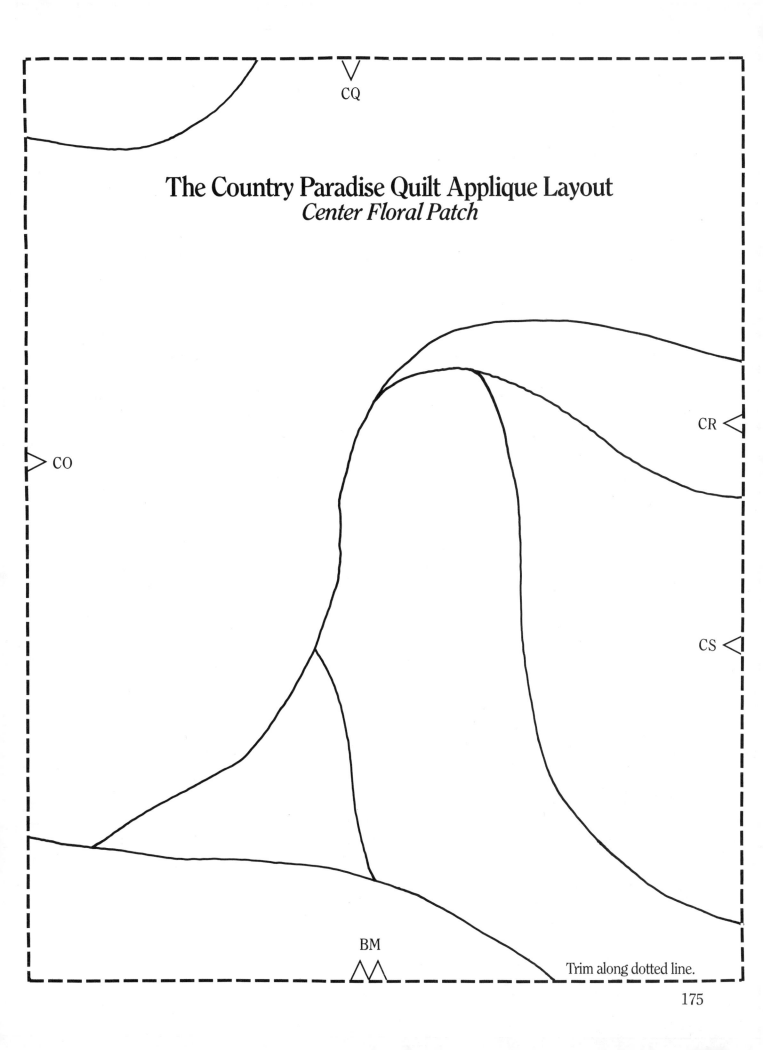

The Country Paradise Quilt Applique Layout
Center Floral Patch

CQ

CO

CR

CS

BM

Trim along dotted line.

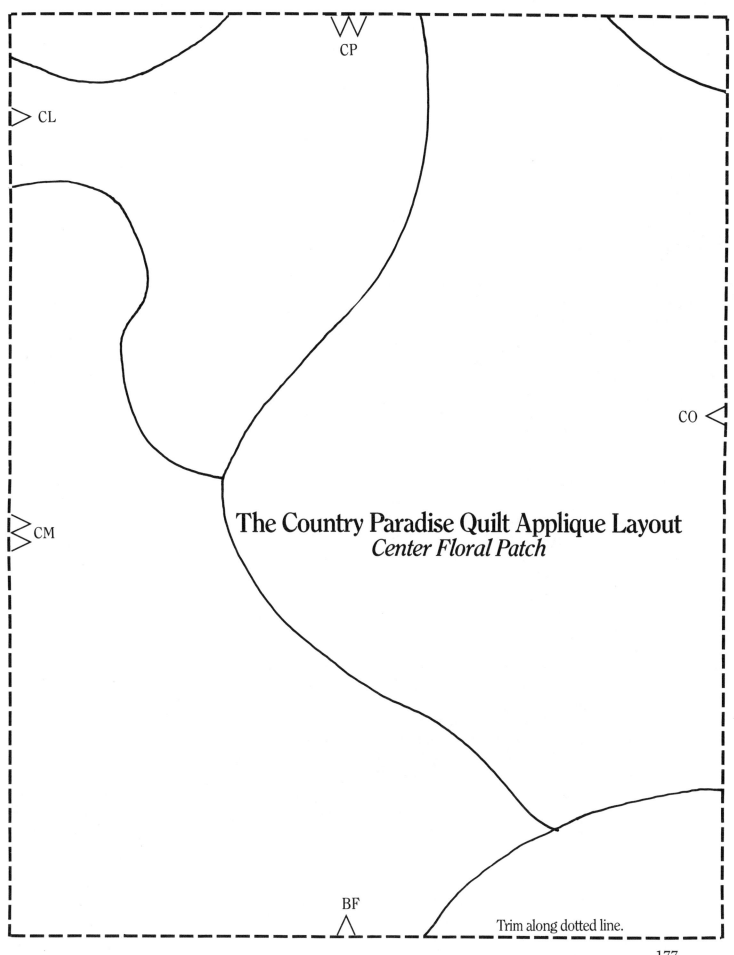

CP

CL

CO

CM

The Country Paradise Quilt Applique Layout
Center Floral Patch

BF

Trim along dotted line.

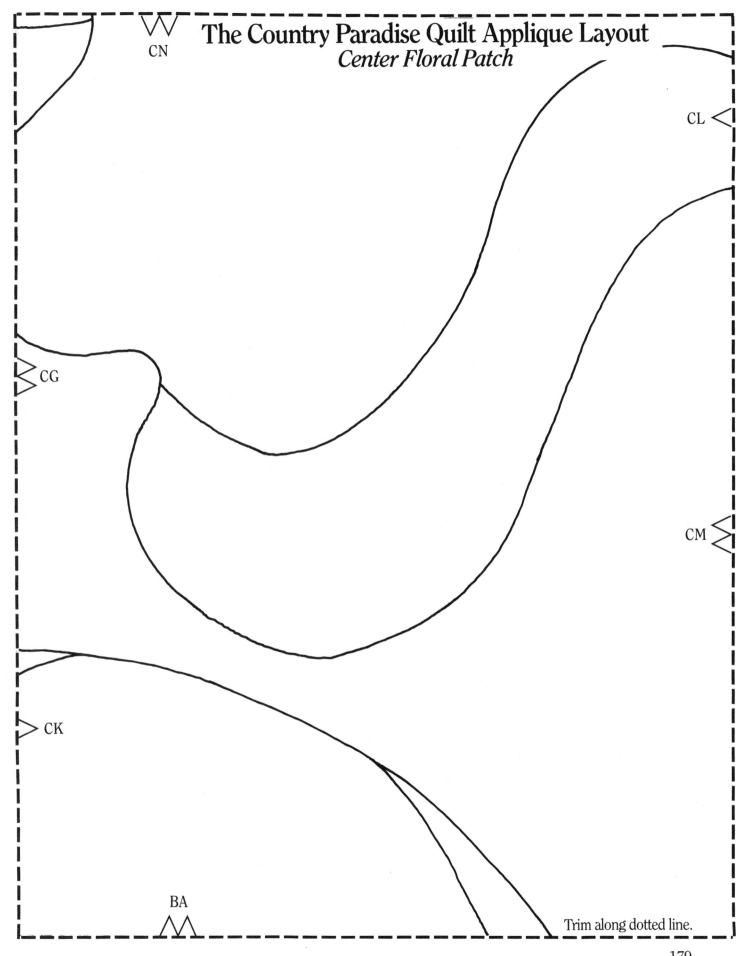

The Country Paradise Quilt Applique Layout
Center Floral Patch

CN

CL

CG

CM

CK

BA

Trim along dotted line.

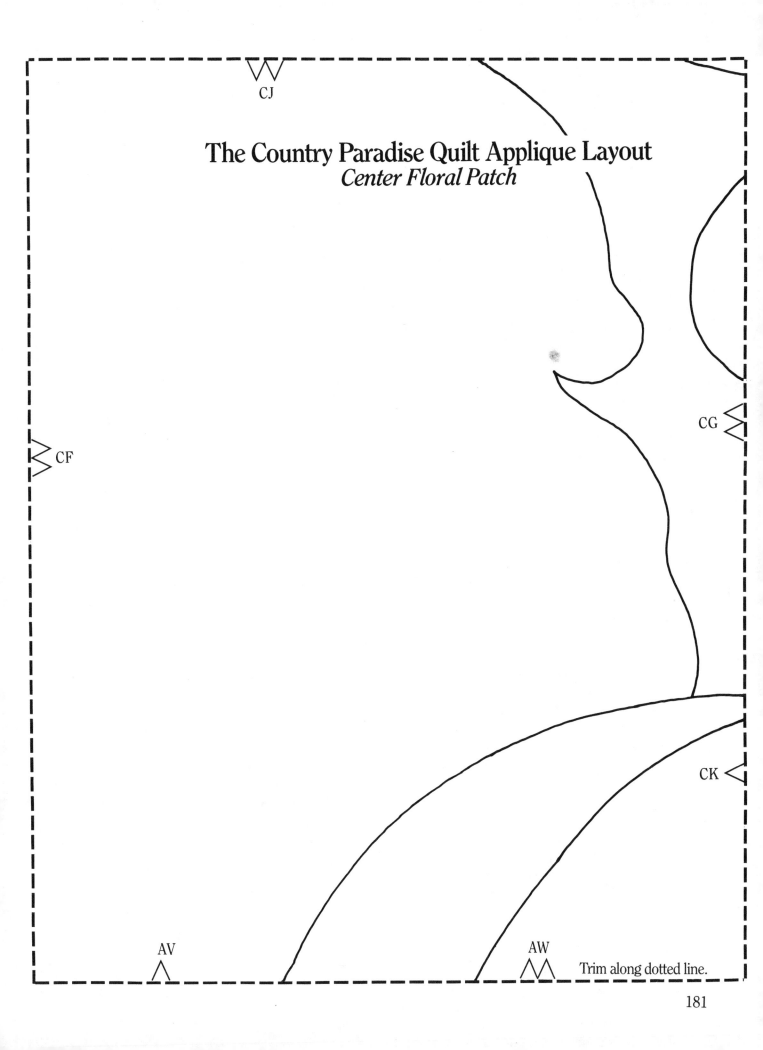

The Country Paradise Quilt Applique Layout
Center Floral Patch

CJ

CF

CG

CK

AV

AW

Trim along dotted line.

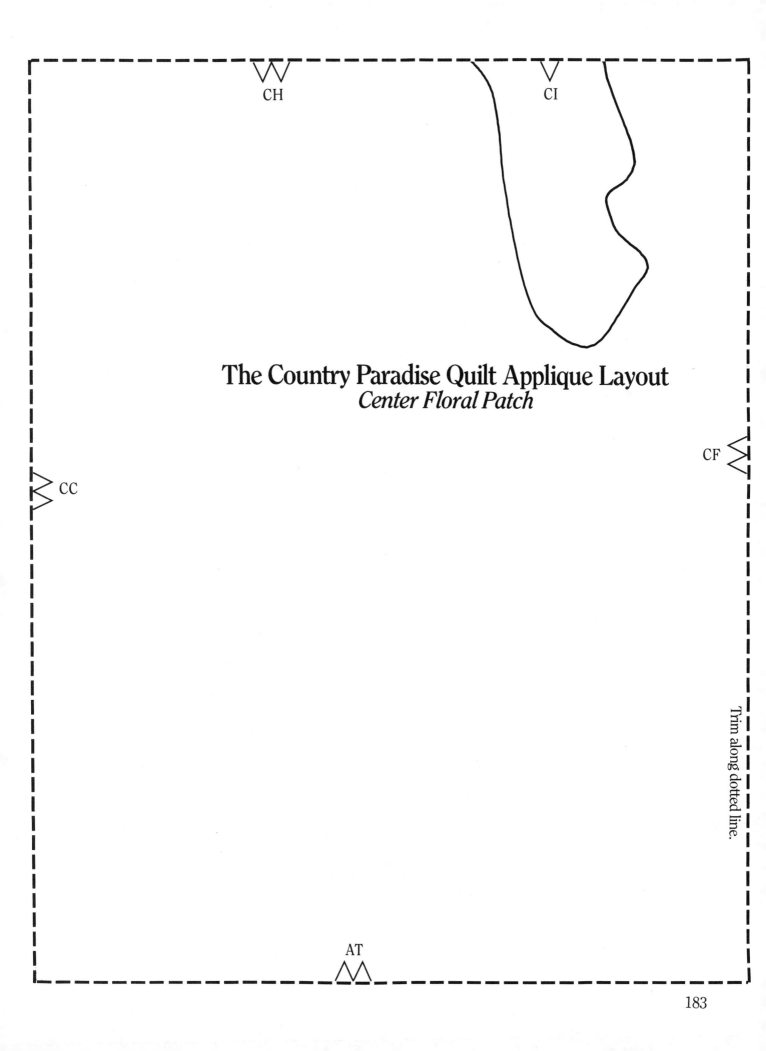

The Country Paradise Quilt Applique Layout
Center Floral Patch

CH

CI

CF

CC

AT

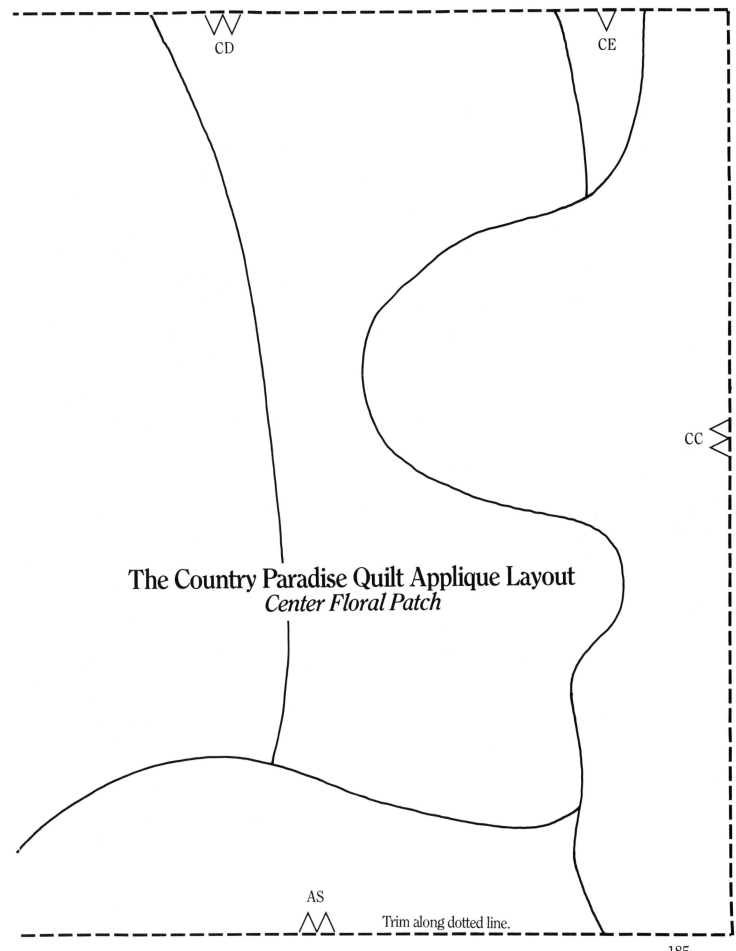

CD

CE

CC

The Country Paradise Quilt Applique Layout
Center Floral Patch

AS

Trim along dotted line.

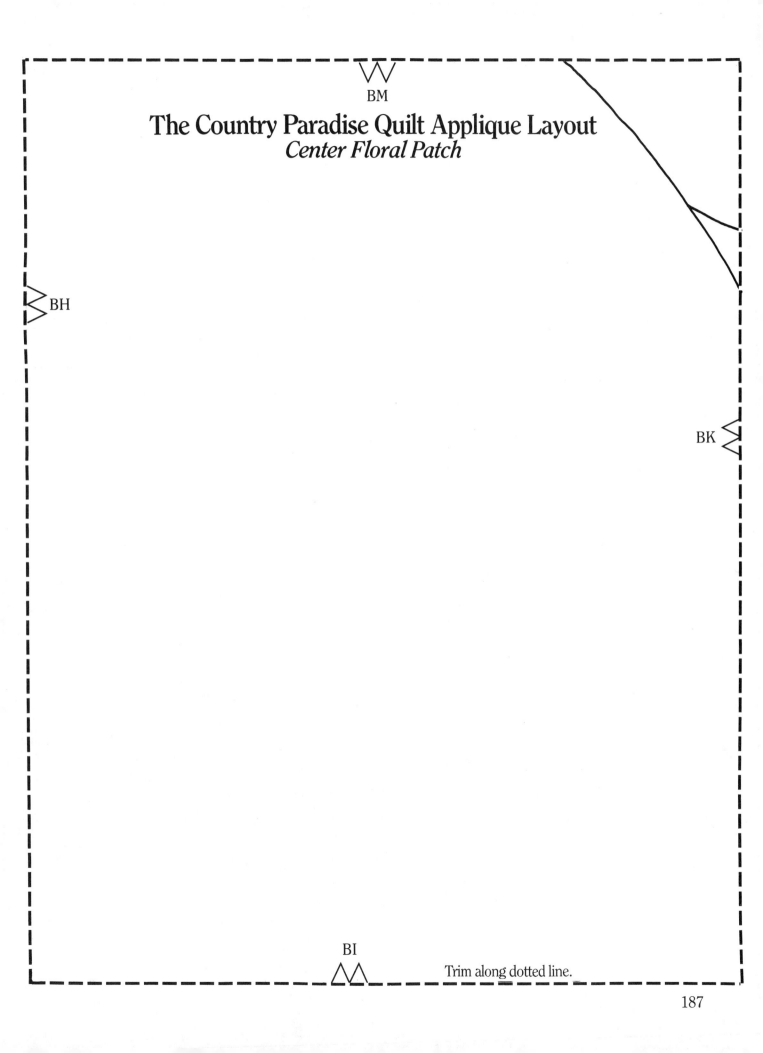

The Country Paradise Quilt Applique Layout
Center Floral Patch

BM

BH

BK

BI

Trim along dotted line.

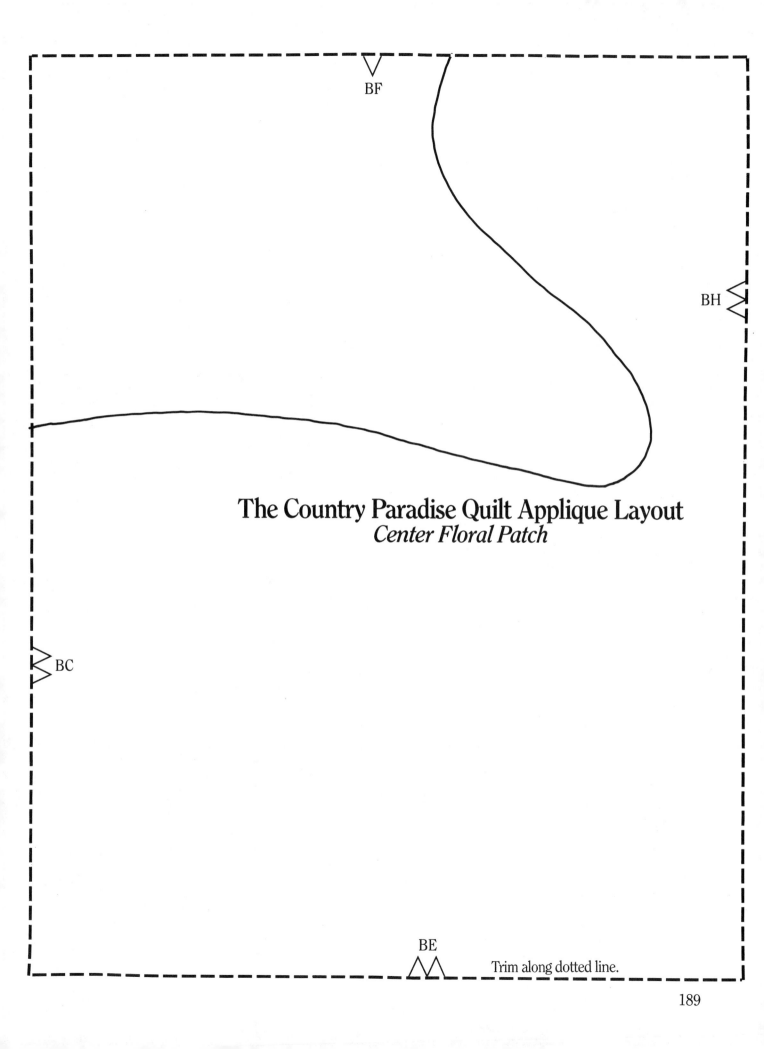

The Country Paradise Quilt Applique Layout
Center Floral Patch

BF

BH

BC

BE

Trim along dotted line.

189

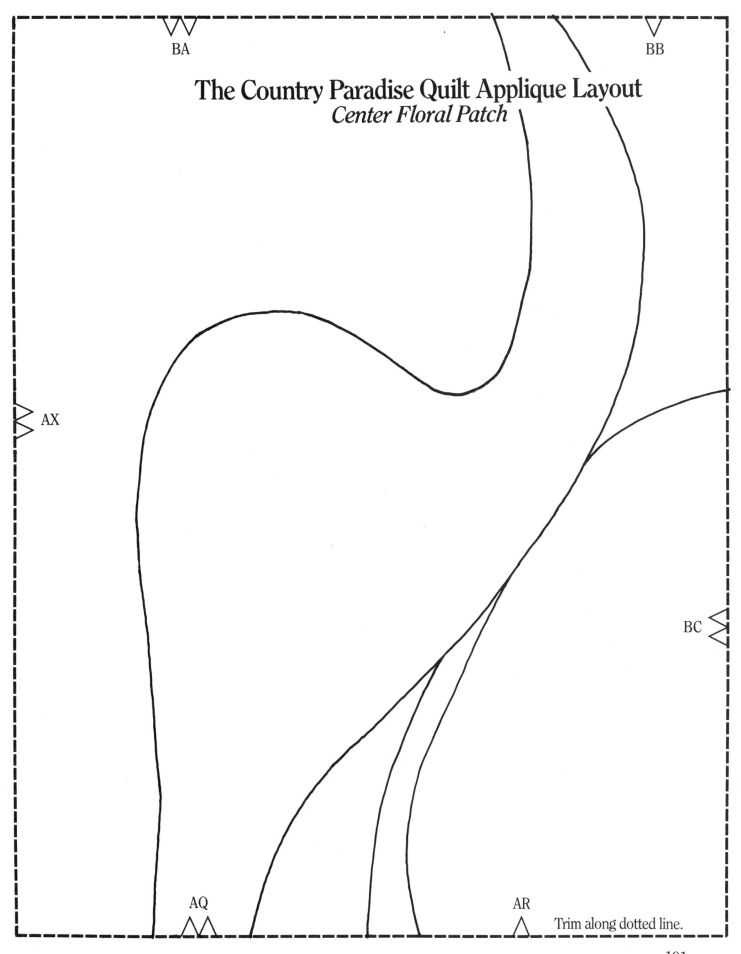

The Country Paradise Quilt Applique Layout
Center Floral Patch

BA

BB

AX

BC

AQ

AR

Trim along dotted line.

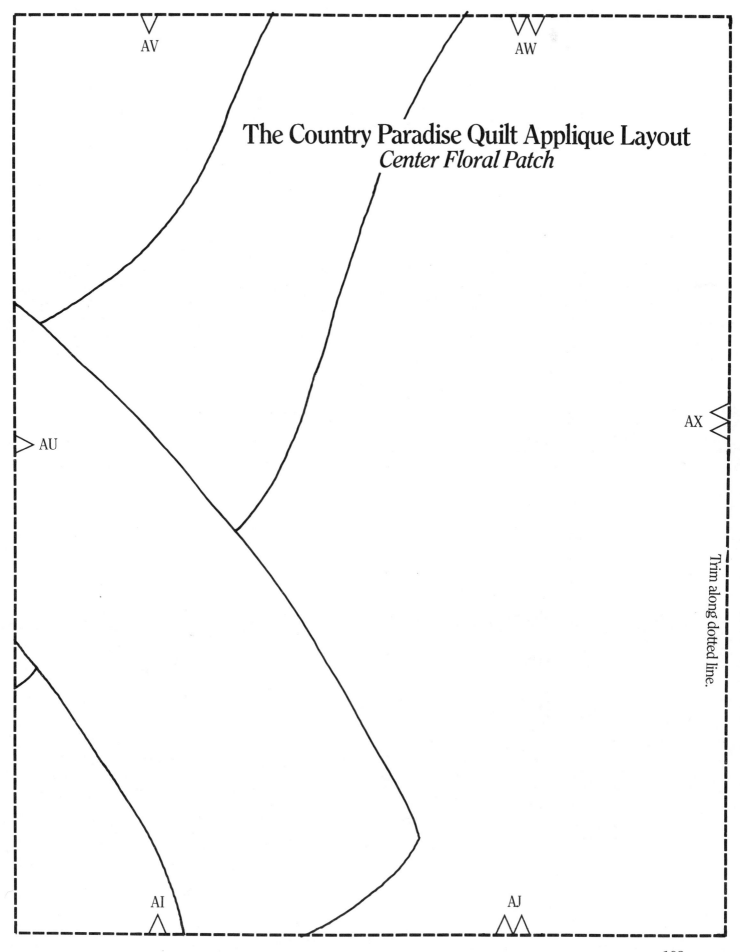

The Country Paradise Quilt Applique Layout
Center Floral Patch

AV

AW

AU

AX

AI

AJ

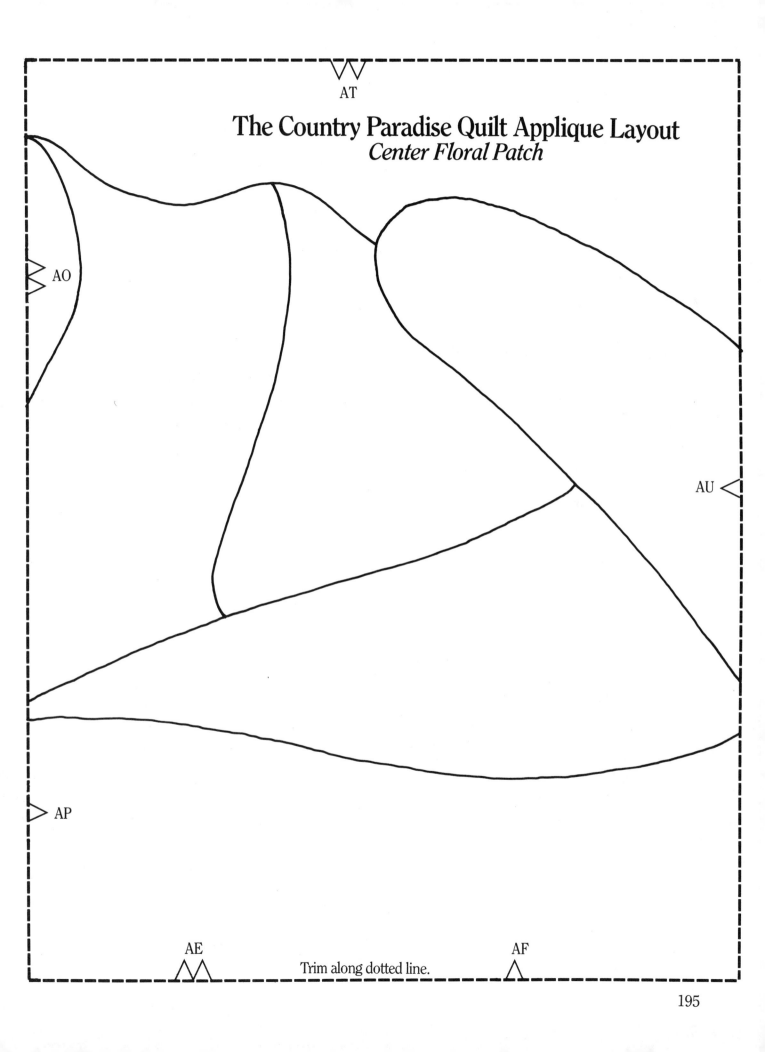

The Country Paradise Quilt Applique Layout
Center Floral Patch

AT

AO

AU

AP

AE

AF

Trim along dotted line.

195

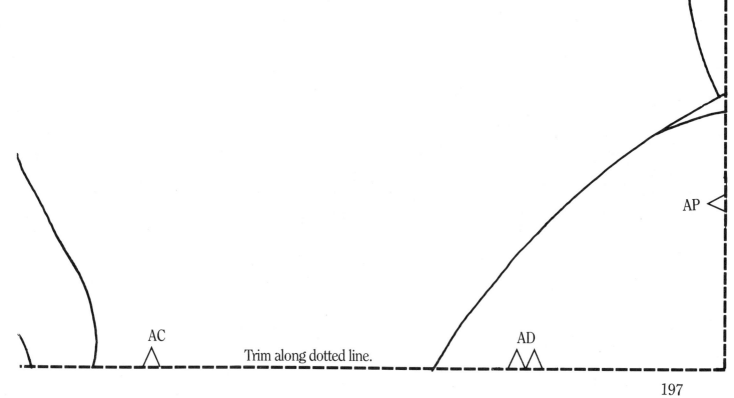

AS

The Country Paradise Quilt Applique Layout
Center Floral Patch

AO

AP

AC

AD

Trim along dotted line.

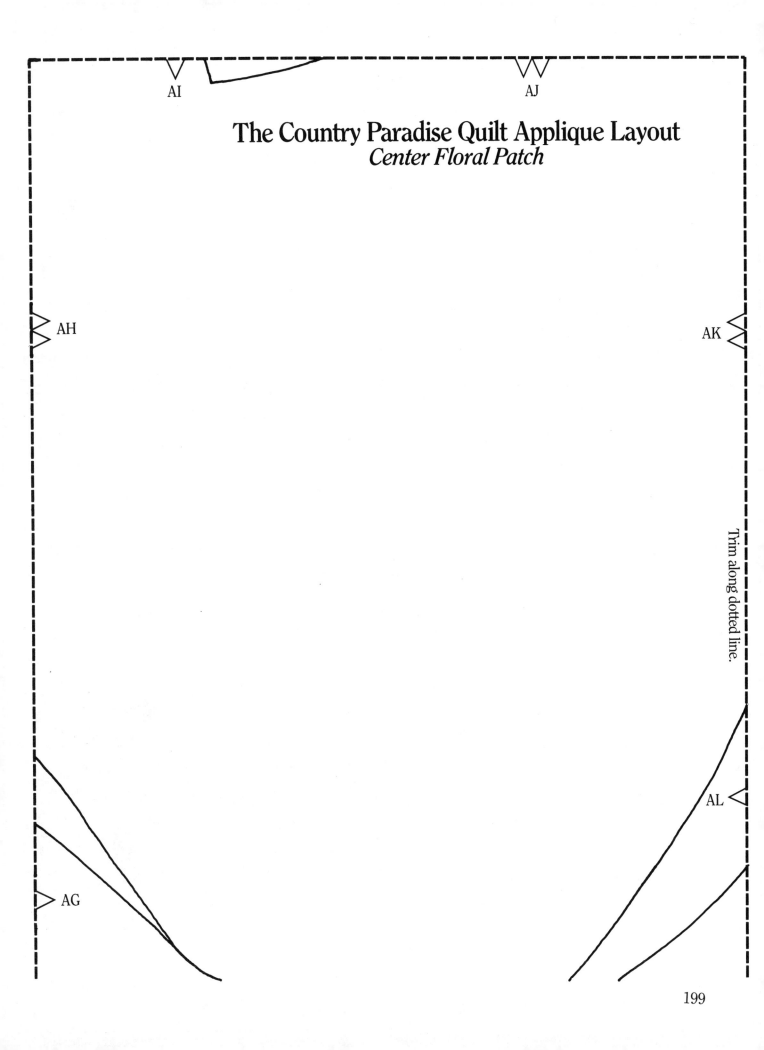

The Country Paradise Quilt Applique Layout
Center Floral Patch

AI

AJ

AH

AK

Trim along dotted line.

AG

AL

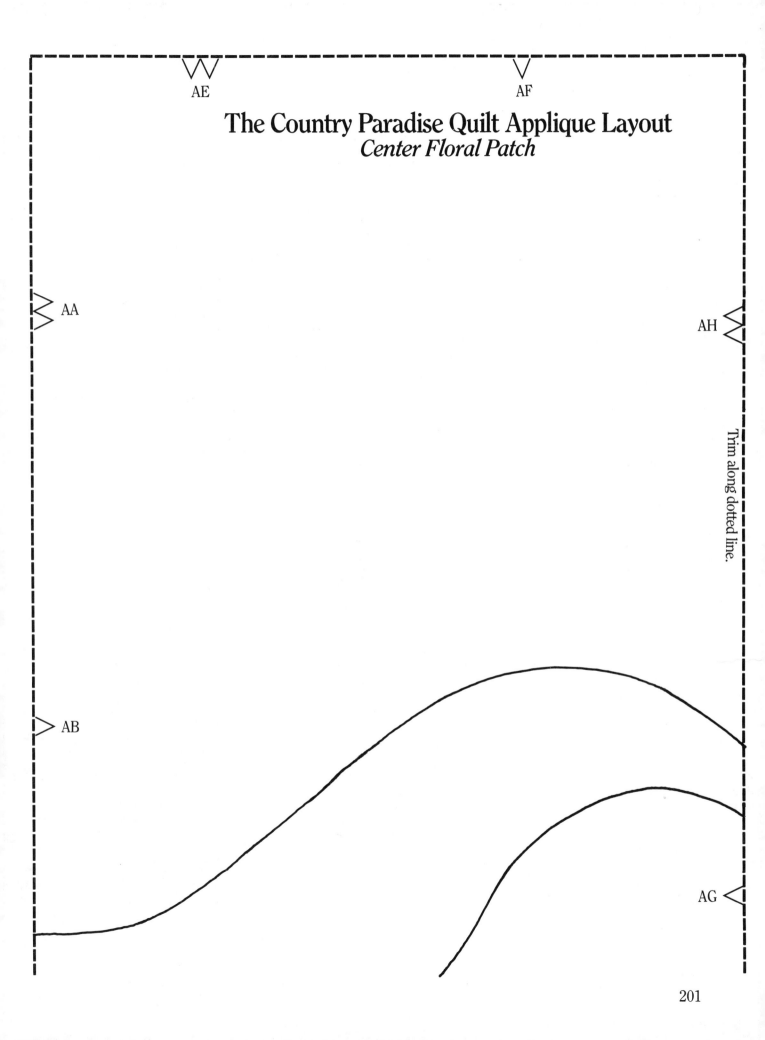

The Country Paradise Quilt Applique Layout
Center Floral Patch

AE

AF

AA

AH

Trim along dotted line.

AB

AG

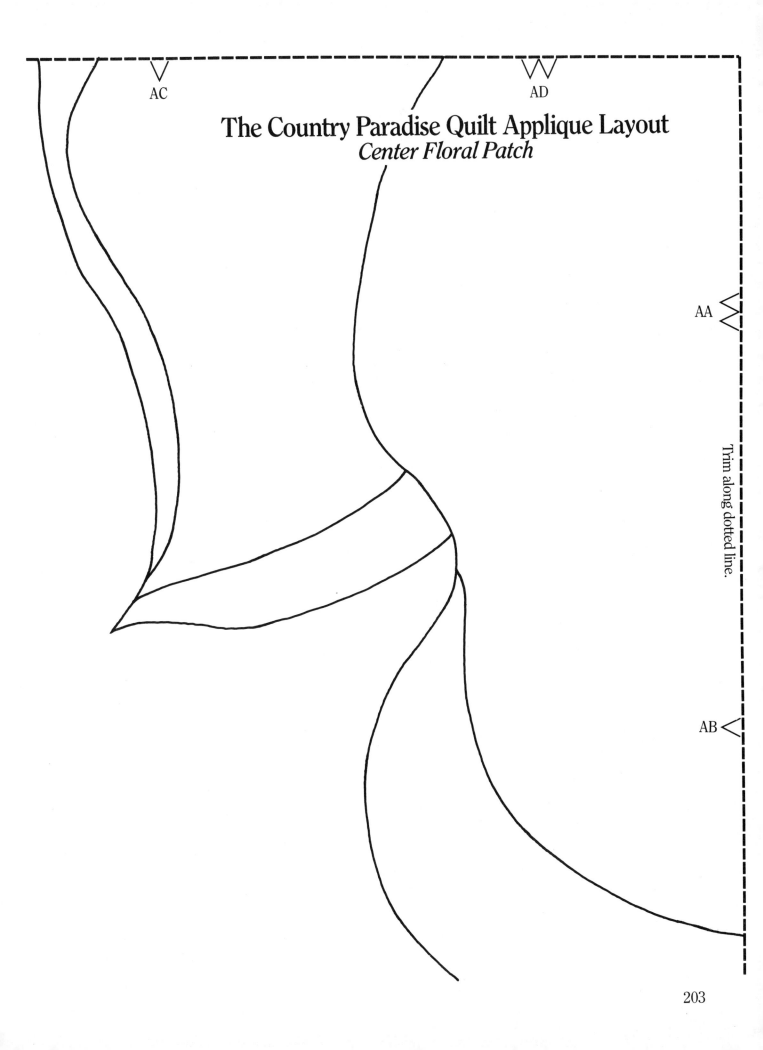

The Country Paradise Quilt Applique Layout
Center Floral Patch

AC

AD

AA

AB

Trim along dotted line.

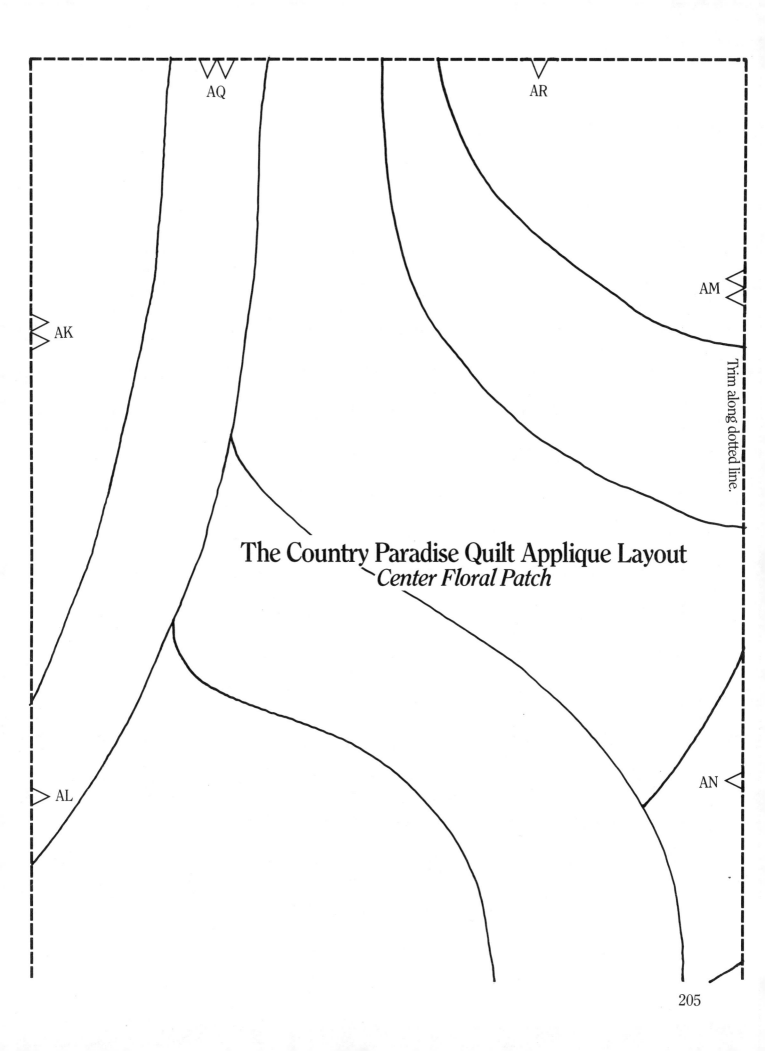

The Country Paradise Quilt Applique Layout
Center Floral Patch

AQ

AR

AM

Trim along dotted line.

AK

AL

AN

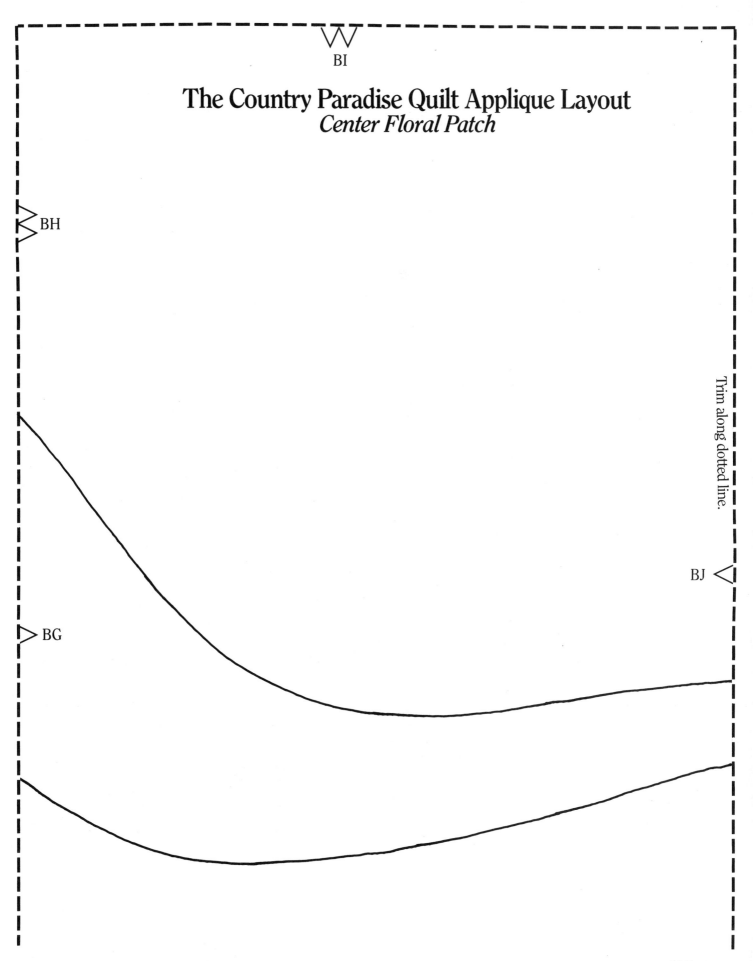

The Country Paradise Quilt Applique Layout
Center Floral Patch

BI

BH

BG

BJ

Trim along dotted line.

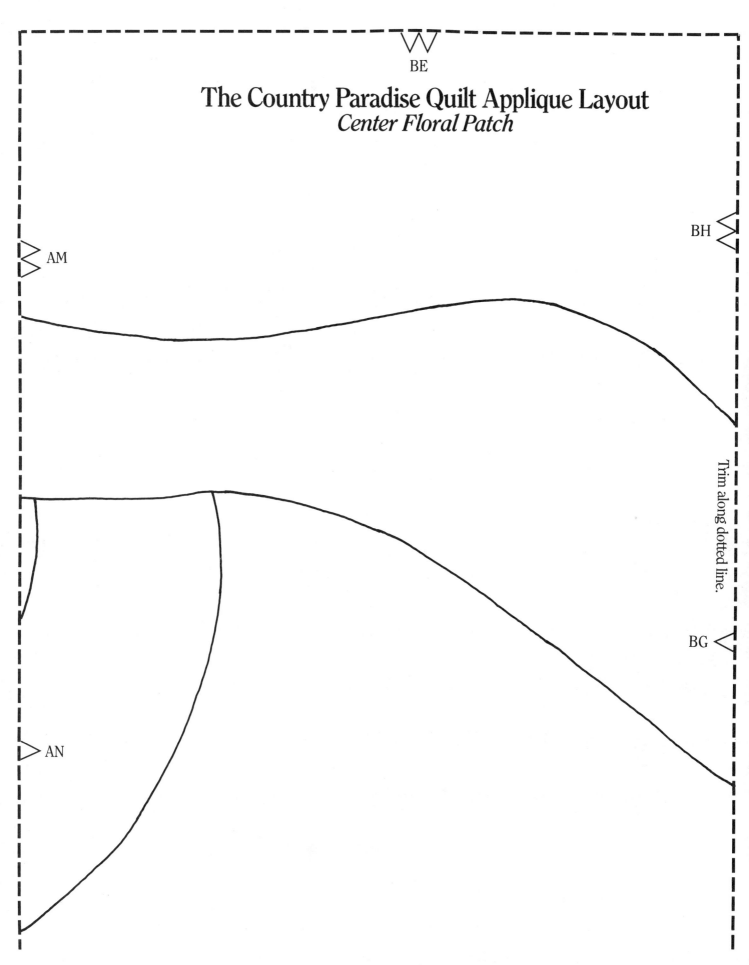

BE

The Country Paradise Quilt Applique Layout
Center Floral Patch

BH

AM

Trim along dotted line.

BG

AN

The Country Paradise Quilt Piecing Templates
Pillow Throw/Nine-Patch Triangle Fan

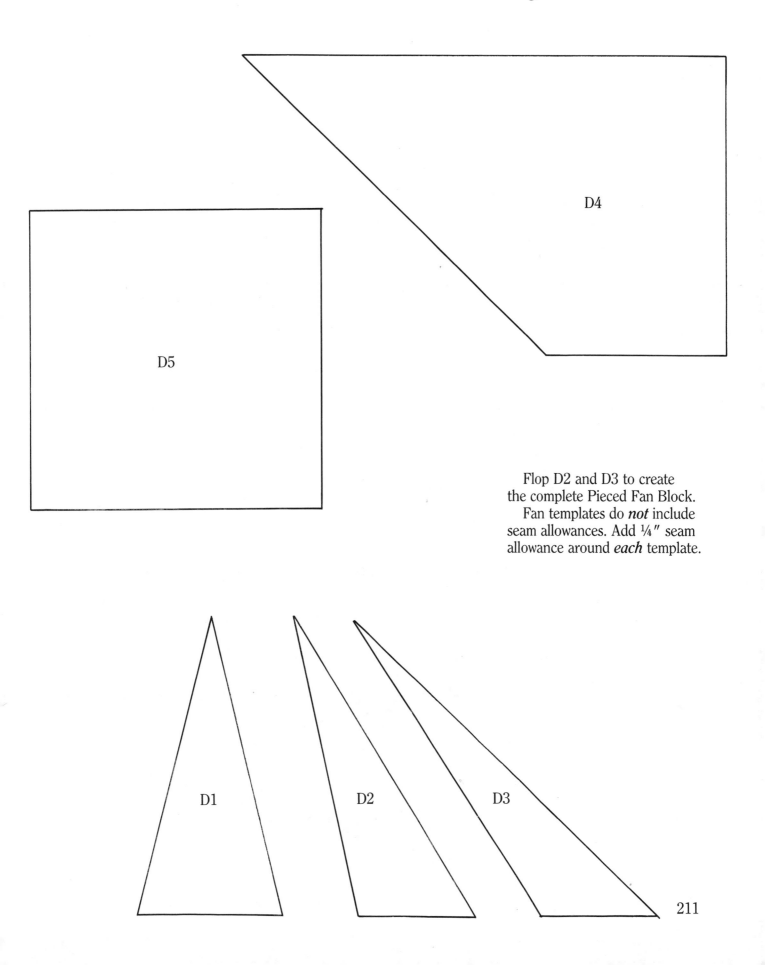

D4

D5

Flop D2 and D3 to create
the complete Pieced Fan Block.
Fan templates do *not* include
seam allowances. Add ¼″ seam
allowance around *each* template.

D1

D2

D3

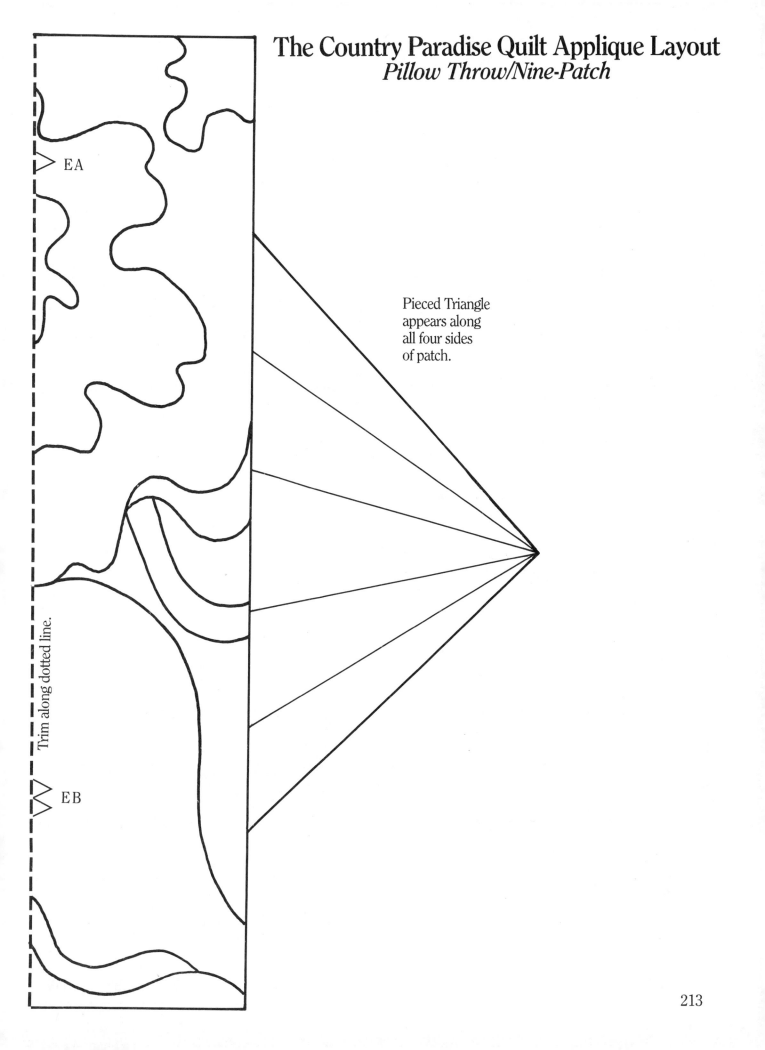

EA

EB

Trim along dotted line.

Pieced Triangle
appears along
all four sides
of patch.

The Country Paradise Quilt Applique Layout
Pillow Throw/Nine-Patch

EA

EB

Trim along dotted line.

215

The Country Paradise Quilt Applique Templates
Pillow Throw/Nine-Patch

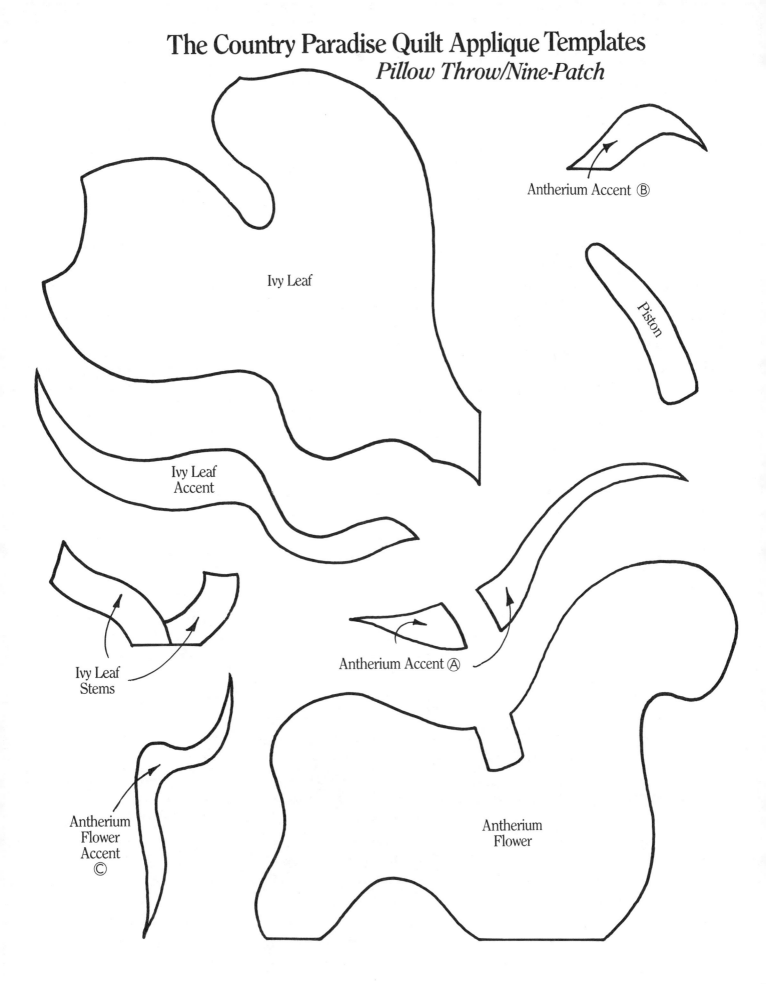

Ivy Leaf

Antherium Accent Ⓑ

Piston

Ivy Leaf
Accent

Ivy Leaf
Stems

Antherium Accent Ⓐ

Antherium
Flower
Accent
Ⓒ

Antherium
Flower

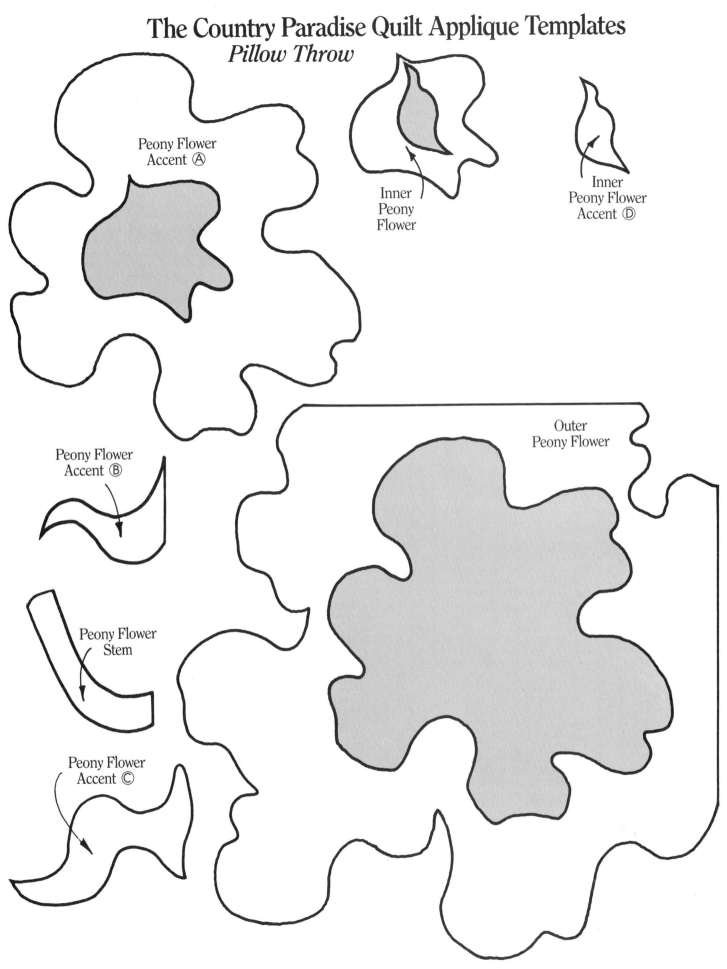

The Country Paradise Quilt Applique Templates
Pillow Throw

Peony Flower
Accent Ⓐ

Inner
Peony
Flower

Inner
Peony Flower
Accent Ⓓ

Peony Flower
Accent Ⓑ

Outer
Peony Flower

Peony Flower
Stem

Peony Flower
Accent Ⓒ

The Country Paradise Quilt Applique Templates

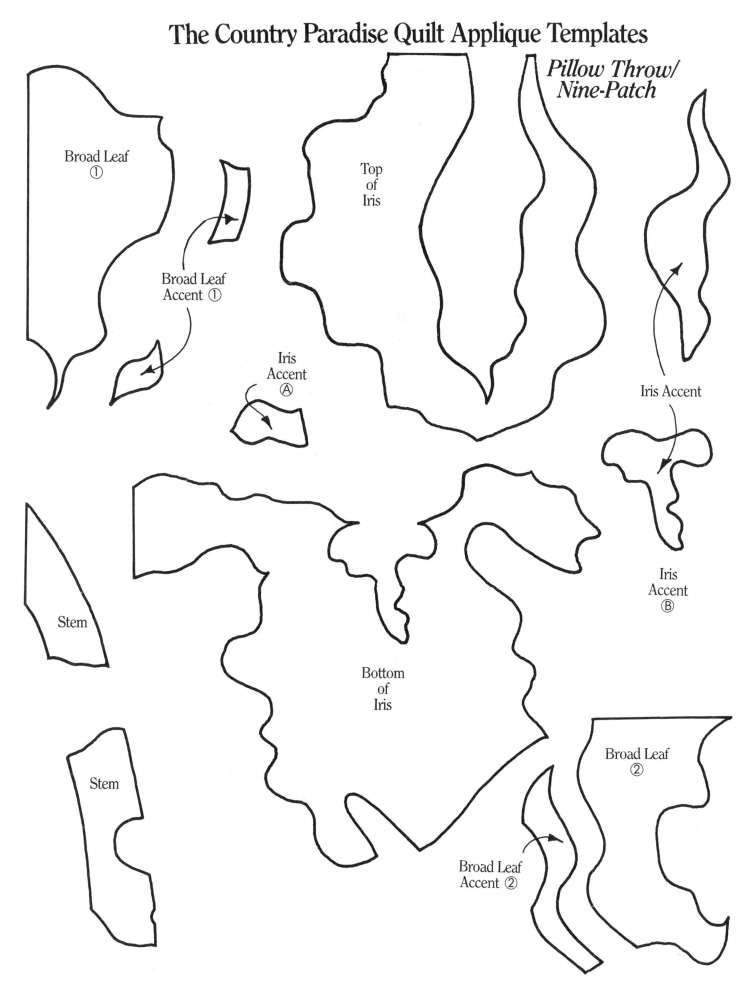

Broad Leaf ①

Broad Leaf Accent ①

Top of Iris

Iris Accent Ⓐ

Iris Accent

Iris Accent Ⓑ

Stem

Bottom of Iris

Stem

Broad Leaf ②

Broad Leaf Accent ②

About The Old Country Store

Cheryl A. Benner and Rachel T. Pellman are on the staff of The Old Country Store, located along Route 340 in Intercourse, Pennsylvania. The Store offers crafts from more than 300 artisans, most of whom are local Amish and Mennonites. There are quilts of traditional and contemporary designs, patchwork pillows and pillow kits, afghans, stuffed animals, dolls, tablecloths and Christmas tree ornaments. Other handcrafted items include potholders, sunbonnets and wooden toys.

For the do-it-yourself quilter, the Store offers quilt supplies, fabric at discount prices, and a large selection of quilt books and patterns.

Located on the second floor of the Store is The People's Place Quilt Museum. The Museum, which opened in 1988, features antique Amish quilts and crib quilts, as well as a small collection of dolls, doll quilts, socks and other decorative arts.

About the Authors

Cheryl A. Benner and Rachel T. Pellman together developed The Country Paradise designs. They created the patterns, then selected fabrics and supervised the making of the original quilts by Lancaster County Mennonite women. This is Benner's and Pellman's fifth collaboration on quilt designs with related books. Their earlier books are the popular *The Country Love Quilt*, *The Country Lily Quilt*, *The Country Songbird Quilt*, and *The Country Bride Quilt Collection*.

Benner, her husband Lamar, and young son live in Honeybrook, Pa. She is a graduate of the Art Institute of Philadelphia (Pa.). Benner is art director for Good Enterprises, Intercourse, Pa.

Pellman lives near Lancaster, Pa., and is manager of The Old Country Store, Intercourse. She is co-author of *The Country Bride Quilt*. She is also the author of *Amish Quilt Patterns* and *Small Amish Quilt Patterns*; co-author with Jan Steffy of *Patterns for Making Amish Dolls and Doll Clothes*; and co-author with her husband, Kenneth, of *A Treasury of Amish Quilts*, *The World of Amish Quilts*, *Amish Crib Quilts*, and *Amish Doll Quilts, Dolls, and Other Playthings*.

The Pellmans are the parents of two sons.